the omega 3 cookbook

Kyle Cathie Ltd

Over 100 smart recipes for body and brain

the OMEGA 3 cookbook

Michael van Straten

with photography by Steve Lee

First published in Great Britain in 2007 by
Kyle Cathie Ltd
122 Arlington Road, London NW1 7HP
general.enquiries@kyle-cathie.com
www.kylecathie.com

10 9 8 7 6 5 4 3 2 1

978 1 85626 707 6

Editorial Director Muna Reyal
Designer Geoff Hayes
Photographer Steve Lee
Home economist Annie Rigg
Styling Jo Harris
Copyeditor Jennifer Wheatley
Proofreader Danielle Di Michiel
Production Sha Huxtable and Alice Holloway

A Cataloguing In Publication record for this title is
available from the British Library.

Colour reproduction by Sang Choy
Printed and bound in Slovenia by MKT PRINT d.d.

IMPORTANT NOTE
The information and advice contained in this book are intended as a
general guide to dieting and healthy eating and are not specific to
individuals or their particular circumstances. This book is not intended
to replace treatment by a qualified practitioner. Neither the author nor
the publishers can be held responsible for claims arising from the
inappropriate use of any dietary regime.

Do not attempt self-diagnosis or self-treatment for serious or long-term
conditions without consulting a medical professional or qualified
practitioner.

ACKNOWLEDGEMENTS

My wife Sally has worked long and hard on developing these omega 3 recipes
and both of us would like to thank Kyle for publishing yet another of our books.
To us she's not just a publisher but a cherished and trusted friend, whose advice
is always welcome.

It's been a joy to work once more with our editor, Muna who, as usual, spots the
gaps, controls my sometimes exuberant fantasies and keeps me focused on the
specific messages of the book.

I've now written more than 40 books and most of the words have been input by
my secretary Janet so as always my thanks go to her too.

I've had two trips on fishing boats – one in the stormy waters of the Irish Sea
and another around the Norwegian cod fisheries. Both were exciting but even in
good conditions, very scary and they made me realise what a huge debt all us
fish eaters have to the trawlermen around the world.

Finally I must mention four academics whose work has put the scientific facts
into my own perceptions of Granny's constant reminders to 'eat your fish, it's
good for your brain'. The first is Professor Michael Crawford at the *Institute of
Brain Chemistry* whom I've known and whose work I've followed for more than
30 years. Second is Dr Artemis P. Simopoulos, a pioneer of essential fatty acid
research. My dear friend and highly respected researcher is Professor Herb
Joiner-Bey, author of the Clinician's Handbook of Natural Medicine, a
naturopathic physician in Washington and a welcome, charming, amazingly
informative and frequent visitor to our home. Finally I must thank Dr Alex
Richardson at Oxford University, the UK's leading authority on the impact of
nutrition and environment on the brain. Her contributions to my radio
programme, her unfailing and excellent scientific advice and her friendship are
all invaluable.

contents

the fats of life

Why, when there is an ever-increasing amount of evidence about the protective, curative and life-enhancing benefits of omega 3 and omega 6 (essential fatty acids or EFAs), do parents, shoppers and eaters get it so wrong?

There are essential fats, good fats, bad fats and middle-of-the-road fats, and throughout the Western world most people consume far too little of the essential fats and far too much of all the others. 'Fat is bad' seems to be the universal message. It gives you heart disease, clogs up your arteries, causes high blood pressure, is linked to breast pain, bowel cancer, obesity and a host of other health horrors. Everywhere you look there are adverts, posters and food labels screaming 'low fat' messages – as if you'd expect your breakfast cereal, a loaf of bread or carton of pure fruit juice to have much fat in the first place.

The real tragedy however is that so many people stop eating what they perceive as 'fatty foods' like oily fish because they link fat with weight gain and poor health. Nothing could be further from the truth. Oily fish, and many other foods like nuts, seeds and some vegetable oils, are vital sources of the omega fatty acids which are essential for life and cannot be manufactured by the body. And too little fat in the diet also means poor absorption of the fat-soluble vitamins A, D, E, and K – essential for natural resistance to infection, healthy skin, eyes, heart and circulation, strong bones and normal blood clotting.

Maximising the omega effect

In this book we'll explore together where to find these wonderful nutrients and how to use them in the creation of delicious, interesting and easily prepared dishes. There are smoothies and salads, fishcakes and frittatas using sardines, mackerel and salmon, and you'll even find unusual foods like flax seeds and purslane (see photograph) in the recipes.

These foods contain essential fatty acids (omega 3 fats) which can help children with learning difficulties and adults with arthritis; they relieve all types of inflammation and help conditions as diverse as dry eye syndrome to ulcerative colitis. All you need to do is find out which foods contain the best forms and how to include enough of them in your diet.

If you're struggling with problem children the answers could be here. The omega fatty acids can revolutionise the lives of parents coping with youngsters who have dyslexia, ADHD and dyspraxia and though this may not be the answer for all youngsters, there is now overwhelming evidence of how increasing their intake of essential fatty acids can result in phenomenal changes. Recent research also suggests that a higher intake has a significant effect on reading skills.

Omega 3 and omega 6 fats don't only play a key role in brain development – they are also some of the most powerful protectors of the heart. You need them to maintain good vision. They're a key to relieving the symptoms of allergies and they can be a powerful tool in creating periods of remission for those suffering from the inflammatory bowel diseases – like Crohn's disease, IBS, colitis and ulcerative colitis. Both adults and children with asthma, eczema and psoriasis can benefit from the anti-inflammatory properties of these unique fats.

If you're planning a baby, pregnant or breast feeding the omega fats become even more important. The vital role of these oils – easily obtained from fatty fish – has been proven time and again, and the fundamental work by Professor Michael Crawford showed that pregnant mums consuming little or no oily fish had babies whose brain and intellectual development was markedly slower than the babies whose mums enjoyed recommended amounts of these foods throughout their pregnancies and breast feeding.

This book is a celebration of the wonderful foods and recipes that provide the highest levels of the essential omega fatty acids. You'll find recipes that perfectly balance the omega 3 and 6s to reduce inflammation and improve the transmission of electrical impulses on which all brain and nerve function depends. For vegetarians and vegans there is advice on getting the best out of seed and plant sources. This is not a book of no's and don'ts, nor is it a prescription for boring diets and unpalatable dishes. Rather it's a festival of fabulous flavours utilising the best possible sources.

a matter of fat

There has been a lot of publicity recently about what the omega fatty acids can do for you and your child. Confusingly, there has also been a lot of contradictory evidence about how much good they can do.

What is a fact is that these fats are essential. Your body cannot manufacture them, but it needs them to keep your skin, nervous system and immune system functioning well.

Omega 3 EFAs are found in cell walls or membranes through which electrical signals travel from brain cell to brain cell. These signals need to pass through the cell walls, but if your body is deficient in omega 3, then the cell walls become less efficient in communicating these signals.

There is also clear evidence that omega 3 EFAs can protect your heart and help inflammatory conditions (including keeping your joints moving) as well as brain function and mood disorders.

For these reasons, omega 3 is especially important for pregnant and breast-feeding women as babies cannot make them either and depend on their mother for their supply. These fatty acids are crucial for the development of a baby's brain and eye development, as well as motor skills.

And although scientists are still exploring the benefits of omega 3 supplements, nobody disputes the importance of including omega-rich foods in your diet. In addition to this, fish is a great source of protein, vitamins and minerals. Fish and seafood used to be a staple part of our diet, but the Western diet has changed so much over the past century that it comes as no surprise that we are deficient in these essential fatty acids.

To find your way through the maze of fat matters, ignore information which obviously comes from sources with vested interests in either promoting or rubbishing the health benefits of any fat or oil. Just stick to the facts. To help you, here's my star guide – five stars for brilliant, four for good, three for okay, two for be careful, one for eat this if you dare!

a little bit of chemistry

ESSENTIAL FATTY ACIDS ★★★★

Essential fatty acids (EFAs) – these are polyunsaturated fats and are liquid at room temperature. There are two groups of EFAs – omega 3 and omega 6 fatty acids. EFAs, as their name suggests, are essential and our bodies cannot manufacture them.

Linoleic, otherwise known as omega 6 fatty acids, are essential for health and are found in most vegetable oils. But you really don't need much of them and excessive amounts can speed up the growth of cancer cells.

Alpha-linolenic, or omega 3 fatty acids are the healthiest of all and they abound in oily fish and some vegetable oils, especially those made from rapeseed, walnuts and flax seeds. Omega 3 not only protects against heart disease and cancer but is very important during pregnancy for the proper formation of the growing baby's brain cells.

Alpha-linolenic acid (ALA) and linoleic acid (LA) are the simplest, but less useful forms of the omega fatty acids – they're found naturally in some nuts, seeds, grains, greens and vegetable oils. The two most important EFAs are eicosapentaenoic acid (EPA) and docosahexaenoic acid (DHA), which are both found in oily fish and seafood. In theory, the body can manufacture all the other omega 3s from ALA and omega 6s from LA, so providing the really essential brain and body fats. Unfortunately, in practice this is a very poor and, for some people, impossible process – especially in men.

What also matters is the proportions of these two fatty acids and the healthiest fats are those which have higher amounts of omega 3 relative to omega 6. Oils with lots of omega 6 and very little omega 3 put you in double jeopardy because of the likely cancer-forming properties of the omega 6s and because they also have a negative effect on the heart protection benefits of omega 3.

CONJUGATED LINOLEIC ACID (CLA) ★★★★

CLA was first discovered just over 20 years ago by Professor Mike Pariza at the University of Wisconsin in the US. At that time, researchers in America were concerned that fried hamburgers might be a potential cause of cancer. Pariza found that this natural fat in beef had powerful anti-cancer properties. But his startling research showed that only free-range cattle raised on natural grasslands actually contained CLA. As well as its anti-cancer properties, this valuable fat stimulates the human body's conversion of stored fats into energy. This is just one more good reason for choosing organic beef, poultry, eggs and dairy products. As a bonus, they will also supply some valuable amounts of the essential omega fatty acids.

POLYUNSATURATED FATS ★★★★

These are all liquid even at low temperatures and extracted from plant sources like sunflowers, safflowers, rapeseed and corn.

Polyunsaturated fats are generally healthier than saturated fats and for many years now polyunsaturated oils and margarines have been linked to healthy heart benefits, but unfortunately it's not that simple. Polyunsaturates have a high content of omega 6 fatty acids in relation to omega 3 and, as you will see, it is the balance between the different types of fat in polyunsaturated oils that is the most important factor. These are rich in the omega 6 fats, but have no omega 3, so the increase in their use means that the balance of the modern Western diet has altered dramatically over the past three or four generations. This means that the relationship between these two components has shifted so much that we now consume four times more 6s than 3s. Even though the omega 6 fats are essential, this ratio has been linked to mental and physical disorders.

MONOUNSATURATED FATS ★★★★

Olive oil is the most commonly used and, although liquid at room temperature, it solidifies if refrigerated. The richest sources are olives, olive oil, avocados, walnuts and walnut oil, peanuts and peanut oil.

Monounsaturated fats are much better for your heart and can even help reduce the amount of cholesterol in your bloodstream. These fats, too, appear to have no role in the formation of cancer.

SATURATED FATS ★★

These are nearly all animal fats from meat and meat products, poultry and associated products like milk, cream, cheese, butter, lard and suet. These fats are all solid at room temperature.

It's these fats that can lead to an increase in cholesterol, which in turn blocks the arteries and causes heart disease and raised blood pressure. Though there's little direct evidence that they play a role in the development of cancer, many experts believe that lower consumption reduce the risks – especially of bowel cancer.

TRANS FATS ★

Trans fats do not occur in nature, but are the result of a catalytic process to solidify the cheapest vegetable oils to use in food manufacturing. The resulting hydrogenated fats are much cheaper than butter and you'll find them in widespread use in take-aways, ready meals, cakes, biscuits, crisps and even in sauces, dressings and 'instant' foods. They crop up most commonly in hard margarines and to a lesser extent in the soft forms too. Margarine manufacturers have recently taken steps to reduce the amounts of trans fats in their products, but watch out for them in pre-packed snack foods.

Trans fats are the ultimate fatty villains and the American Department of Health has recently legislated to force manufacturers to declare the content of trans fats on food labels. Dr Michael Jacobson, executive director of the Washington-based Center for Science in the Public Interest, has been campaigning against trans fats for years. He has always maintained that the safe limit for a day's consumption is nil. Now, the US government and the New York Board of Health agrees. Consuming these trans fats carries a significantly higher risk of causing heart disease – higher even than saturated fats, like the crackling on pork, skin on crispy duck or the layer on the outside of your lamb chop. There is some evidence that trans fats are also linked to an increased risk of breast cancer.

the best oils to use regularly

OLIVE OIL ★★★★★

This is one of the healthiest of culinary oils as it helps to reduce blood levels of cholesterol, contains lots of monounsaturates and is low in omega 6.

RAPESEED, WALNUT AND FLAX-SEED OIL ★★★★★

All these have very low amounts of saturated fatty acids, substantial monounsaturates and a good balance between the omega 3 and omega 6 fatty acids.

COCONUT AND PALM OILS ★

These contain large amounts of saturated fats, little mono-unsaturated fat and virtually no omega 3, so they're best avoided. When buying foods tinned in oil, steer clear of products labelled 'vegetable oil' – they're almost certain to contain unhealthy coconut or palm oils.

To protect your heart and circulation and minimise your cancer risk, most people need to reduce their overall consumption of fats. The healthiest option for the average person is to reduce saturated and trans fats and use more of the natural, unrefined and, where possible, cold-pressed sources of monounsaturated and the best of the polyunsaturated oils.

Don't go overboard with sunflower oil. Although it has been much publicised as a healthy alternative, especially in cooking, don't use it with abandon. It has more than 60 per cent of omega 6 and virtually no omega 3. True, it's extremely low in saturated fats, but the high levels of omega 6 mean you should use it sparingly.

why **omega oils** are so important

Omega 3 fatty acids are called essential fatty acids because that's exactly what they are. They have two distinct roles, the first of which is in the growth, development and function of the brain and central nervous system. The second is to help with the regulation of chemical processes in the body, to counter inflammatory conditions and to aid the prevention and help relieve the symptoms of an extraordinary range of health problems.

It's difficult to believe that this group of natural substances which the body needs in such small amounts can have such a huge impact on human intellectual, cognitive and physical well-being. As a naturopath, I have been using these amazing fats in the treatment of patients for more than 30 years. As with so many other forms of nutritional therapy, complementary practitioners have grasped their significance and been willing to use them in practice long before the orthodox medical community. After all, we are not looking at some new drug with the potential to produce catastrophic side effects even after it has been through all the regulatory hoops. But orthodoxy requires ever increasing standards of proof even when the evidence of benefit is enormous and the risks of harm non-existent.

Sadly, it's only recently that medicine started to look seriously at the essential fatty acids, even though eminent researchers have been investigating and publishing exciting results for years. It seems extraordinary that diseases from Alzheimer's to rheumatoid arthritis, blood pressure to eczema, dyslexia to ADHD and a host of others in between, could all be helped simply by eating a few sardines or taking a fish oil supplement on a regular basis.

The omega effect

Increasing your consumption of foods rich in omega 3s affects your body in two basic ways: firstly, by reducing the effect of some damaging processes and secondly, by increasing the production of protective chemicals. A key benefit is the ability of fatty acids to reduce and control inflammation. This is just as effective in the relief of inflammatory joint pain as it is in reducing the body's production of cytokines, a group of chemicals which trigger the inflammation closely linked with atherosclerosis (the thickening and hardening of arteries).

A lowered risk of blood clots, reduction of cholesterol and triglycerides in the blood, improved responses to insulin and a better regulation of metabolism and body weight can all be attributed to foods richest in essential fatty acids. There is even emerging evidence that they may help prevent the growth of cancerous cells.

what EFAs can do for you

Our body's survival depends on the ability of cells to function efficiently. Each one needs to be able to get nutrients and eliminate waste products. These two operations are entirely dependent on the condition of the membrane surrounding each cell. Since these membranes are manufactured from fats, what you eat can determine their state of health. A high intake of trans and saturated fats – solid at room temperature – reduces the efficiency of the membranes.

If your diet is rich in EFAs, the membranes do their job and the result is healthier cells which are able to communicate with each other more effectively. This is a vital factor as it seems likely that, without good intercell communication, there is an increased risk of cancer, specifically of the breast. Research published in the *International Journal of Cancer* in 2005 showed that mice implanted with breast cancer cells had a 20–25 per cent reduction of tumour growth when they were fed on a diet rich in omega 3 fish oil, compared to those fed on a diet rich in omega 6 corn oil.

One key to the benefits of omega 3 EFAs is their ability to reduce and control inflammation. This effect can be either direct or indirect, but the end result is safe and beneficial. It now appears that the body manufactures a group of powerful anti-inflammatory chemicals called resolvins directly from EPA. These seem to control the movement of inflammatory cells and substances which are normally attracted to sites of inflammation. These resolvins appear free from side effects, especially the sometimes catastrophic damage caused by non-steriodal anti-inflammatory drugs (NSAIDs) and the new class of NSAID, Cox-2 inhibitors, which can not only damage the digestive system, but have also caused many unexpected deaths from heart problems.

Indirectly, EPA and DHA (the EFAs found in oily fish) trigger the release of the good prostaglandins that stimulate circulation,

lower the risk of blood clots and are potent anti-inflammatories. It's hardly surprising that the traditional use of marine extracts has proved so effective in the relief of arthritic joint pain.

One of the most widely publicised benefits of EFAs is their importance as a key nutrient in developing and maintaining cognitive mental processes, which has led to their growing use in the treatment of conditions across the whole autistic spectrum. They're vital during pregnancy, breast feeding and infancy and, for some children, a valuable treatment option in dyslexia, dyspraxia and ADHD. EFAs have been shown to improve IQ, concentration and memory; to help with depression; to delay symptoms in the early stages of Alzheimer's disease; and even to be of some possible help in the treatment of schizophrenia. Many leading scientists are currently researching the importance of these amazing food constituents. The results and possible benefits of using this type of kitchen medicine are all the more tantalising when related to simple changes in everyday eating habits.

When the outcome can be so good, the downside so negligible and all you have to do is eat the fabulous food in the recipes in this book, the potential benefits are there for the taking. But more about these later.

So how do you know if you need more

The simple answer is that pretty nearly everyone needs more as the consumption of oily fish, nuts, seeds, the best type of oils and virtually all the plant sources of omega 3 is worryingly poor.

There are some very obvious signs that both children and adults may not be getting enough essential fatty acids, but few parents and, sadly, even fewer doctors make the connection as it's all too easy to treat each problem separately unless you take a truly holistic overview.

Dry, scaly skin patches, dandruff, dry and lifeless hair, precipitous and unexplainable mood swings, poor sleep, nails that flake and are always soft, inability to concentrate, eyes that are dry and sore, ADHD (which happens to adults as well as children) – any of these problems can crop up individually, but two or three of them cropping up together are a pretty good indication of omega 3 deficiency. Before rushing into bogus allergy testing, extreme exclusion diets, counselling, psychiatric assessments or, at the very worse, Ritalin (for ADHD) it's important to try improving your diet and using fish oil supplements or flax-seed oil if you're a determined veggie or vegan, but it's not quite the same.

Most of these conditions are chronic and will have been apparent for some time before anyone decides to intervene.

It's very rare that taking a few more weeks to try these very simple and absolutely safe dietary measures would put anyone's health in jeopardy.

Certainly anyone with heart disease, type 2 diabetes, arthritis or any other chronic muscle pain would benefit from increasing the amount of omega 3-rich foods in their diet as well as looking at the balance of omega 3 and omega 6. The same is true if you have dry, itchy skin or eczema, chronic fatigue, depression or loss of concentration. If any of these apply to you, you can make a substantial difference to your quality of life simply by eating salmon, herrings, sardines, flax seeds, walnuts and the wide range of other omega 3-rich foods (see pages 20–21) that you'll find in all the recipes in this book as well as taking a fish oil supplement (page 26).

the balance between omega 3 and 6

It never ceases to amaze me that, in spite of being an island race, with some of the world's finest fish around our coastline and in our lakes and rivers, the consumption of all types of fish has declined drastically over the last 50 years. This is a nutritional and health disaster for a number of reasons.

They have been replaced by a whole range of processed, manufactured meat products, which means a substantial increase in the consumption of saturated fats and an extremely worrying drop in the national levels of vitamin D. This hormone-like nutrient is not only essential for the absorption of calcium from food, which is then used to build strong bones, but it also plays many other roles in the complex chemical processes that occur constantly within the body. This is not a widely available vitamin except from oily fish and, assuming the necessary daily dose to be 10mcg, a small 100g portion of these fish can provide up to 200 per cent of this requirement.

Another disastrous result of these changes in our diet means extremely low intakes of the omega 3 essential fatty acids. Amongst all the health problems related to omega 3 deficiencies, you can include fatigue and exhaustion and this is inevitably aggravated by a lack of iodine – of which fish is the only major source – also linked to the changing balance of the national diet.

On the other side of the scale, there is an ever-increasing consumption of foods with high levels of the omega 6 fatty acids and although these have a vital role to play too, when the ratio of 3 to 6 gets out of kilter the problems begin. Fifty years ago the 3 to 6 average was 1:4, which most nutritional experts regard as ideal. Today it's 1:16 – a 400 per cent increase in the relative levels of omega 6.

From this it's easy to see that the majority of people are much more likely to be deficient in omega 3 than omega 6. The enormous commercial pressures of the advertising of vegetable oils and margarines and the widespread use of vegetable oils and hydrogenated fats has resulted in compounding the problems of too little omega 3 and even more heavily skewing the balance in favour of omega 6. But why does it matter since they're both essential fatty acids?

Correcting body chemistry

It matters because disturbing the balance in this way also changes your body's chemistry, creating a higher risk of heart disease, circulatory problems and inflammatory diseases of the joints and digestive system. The combination of too little omega 3s and much too much omega 6s can also affect your memory, concentration, reasoning and other mental faculties.

Achieving a healthy omega 3 to 6 balance is not difficult as long as you make some simple changes to the way you eat, learn to read the labels and develop a keen eye to help you interpret the information they provide. The first, easiest and most obvious step is to increase the amount of all fish and shellfish in your diet, but especially to eat at least three portions a week of the oily fish – we'll look at the question of toxicity on page 19. At the same time, try to make a substantial reduction in the amount of processed vegetable oils for cooking and dressings as they're the richest sources of omega 6 – see my guide on page 11 for the best oils to use.

One of the worst culprits to watch out for on the labels is 'vegetable oil' as this will inevitably be the cheapest commercial mixture of highly refined oils, which will certainly have a high content of omega 6 but may also contain harmful saturated and trans fats. The other key phrase on food labels which should repel you like garlic repels Dracula is 'hydrogenated fats.' These are, without doubt, one of the least healthy and most widely used ingredients in convenience foods, ready meals, desserts, salad dressings and a whole range of bakery goods.

Just making these simple changes could have a major impact on your health and quality of life and would, without doubt, help reduce your risk of chronic illness as you age. If you're a woman and thinking of starting a family, addressing the question of your omega 3 to 6 balance must be an integral part of your pre-conceptual planning and your dietary regime throughout pregnancy and breast feeding.

how much should you eat?

Unfortunately, the body doesn't find it easy to make its own EPA and DHA so we have to get them from our food. The good news is that plankton – a simple sea organism – can perform this trick. Millions of small fish use plankton, which can make their own omega 3, as their food, so the essential fatty acids end up in their flesh. When bigger fish eat the smaller fish, they get these nutrients too. And when we eat the bigger fish we subsequently get the benefit of the original omega 3s.

Experts vary in their estimation of the optimum consumption of omega 3 fatty acids; the advice ranges from 350mg to 600mg a day. The consensus from those specialists for whom I have the highest regard is that we should all aim for around 500mg, which is a surprisingly small amount, totalling 3.5g a week. However, the latest advice from the nutrition department at the world famous Tufts University in America recommends 7 to 11g of omega 3 fatty acids a week. And one study looking only at the benefits of preventing second heart attacks and sudden death found that a total of 6g a week was an effective dose. According to the Tufts' report, higher doses may be important for the prevention of many health problems, as well as heart disease. These nutrients play a role in the relief of rheumatoid arthritis and cancer prevention as well as improving mood and memory.

I believe that we should all aim at getting a good 6-7g of the omega 3 fatty acids every single week. These are such safe nutrients that there are no recommendations for maximum doses and the only reported drug interaction has been with blood-thinning drugs like Warfarin. Omega 3 fats help the cardio-vascular system because they make the blood less sticky so reducing the risk of clotting. For this reason, they could increase the effect of blood-thinning drugs – possibly resulting in bleeding. If you're taking this type of drug or are on any other prescribed medication, it would be advisable to speak to your doctor before making significant changes in your consumption of omega 3s, particularly if you're considering taking fish oil supplements.

what about pollution?

Eating oily fish is the surest way to guarantee you'll be giving your body all the omega 3s it needs and enough to provide the additional protective benefits. Sadly, living in the 21st century, we are faced with the cumulative problems of the pollution which pervades our world. Even the great oceans have been affected, as well as seas, lakes and rivers. Consequently there are concerns about the contamination of some fish.

Heavy metals like mercury, and toxic organic chemicals like dioxin have been found in some oily fish. Naturally, this raises some concerns. The larger the fish, the higher up the food chain they are and the more toxins they absorb.

The UK Food Standards Agency, like the American authorities, has revised its advice on oily fish. It recommends that children under 16, women planning pregnancy and women who are pregnant or breast feeding should avoid eating shark, marlin and swordfish. It also suggests not more than four medium-sized tins or two fresh tuna steaks a week for pregnant women or those planning to become pregnant.

However, the FSA also says that the popular everyday favourites, like cod, haddock and plaice, are not a problem, nor are the small oily fish like mackerel, herrings, pilchards, sardines, trout and salmon.

In real terms, this means at least three portions of fish every week, two of which should be oily fish – more if you're using the uncontaminated small ones – is a perfectly safe regime, with enormous health benefits.

There are other sources of omega 3s, but most of these non-fish foods contain only small amounts. Use them to top up your consumption and to guarantee that your diet always has a surplus of these vital substances.

For the greater good
In October 2006, *The Journal of the American Medical Association* published the results of a government-funded study by the American Institute of Medicine and the results of an investigation by scientists at the Harvard School of Public Health.

Dariush Mozaffarin, a cardiologist at Harvard, said: 'Farmed salmon has more than twice the amount of omega 3s than wild salmon, yet both are very high. Dioxin and polychlorinated biophenyls can be lower in wild fish than farmed. Overall levels of dioxin and PCBs are low in all fish and, more importantly, the magnitude of the omega 3 benefits is so much greater than any risk from other contaminants.'

good fish sources

To make things simple, the following charts are a practical guide to the amount of oily fish and other foods that will provide at least your optimum daily 1g of omega 3:

FOOD	PORTION
Kippers	30g
Anchovies	30g
Mackerel (fresh)	50g
Mackerel (tinned in oil, drained)	50g
Herrings	50g
Sprats	50g
Pilchards (fresh)	50g
Huss	50g
Salmon (fresh or frozen, raw or cooked)	75g
Salmon (tinned and drained)	50g
Sardines (tinned in oil, drained)	75g
Tuna (fresh)	100g
Tuna (tinned and drained)	350g
Trout (fresh)	100g
Shrimps	100g
Crab (fresh)	100g
Halibut	175g
Mussels (shelled weight)	200g
Oysters	200g
Cod	225g
Scallops (shelled weight)	225g
Lobster (shelled weight)	310g
Barramundi	1,000g

non-fish sources of omega 3

FOOD	QUANTITY	OMEGA 3 content in grams	FOOD	QUANTITY	OMEGA 3 content in grams
Nuts and seeds			**Oils**		
Walnuts	25g	2.6	Flax seed	15ml (1 tbsp)	6.9
Pumpkin seeds	25g	2	Walnut	15ml (1 tbsp)	1.4
Flax seeds	25g	1.8	Rapeseed (canola)	15ml (1 tbsp)	1.3
Pecans (dry roasted)	25g	0.3	Soya bean	15ml (1 tbsp)	0.9
Pine nuts	25g	0.25	Wheatgerm	15ml (1 tbsp)	0.8
Mustard seeds	25g	0.2			
Pistachios	25g	0.1	**Others**		
Poppy seeds	25g	0.1	Purslane	100g	0.4
Sesame seeds	25g	0.1	Pumpkin/squash	100g	0.34
Hazelnuts	25g	trace	Tofu	100g	0.3
Cashews	25g	trace	Cloves (ground)	10g	0.2
Almonds	25g	trace	Chard	100g	0.2
Brazil nuts	25g	trace	Oregano (dried)	2 tbsp	0.12
			Strawberries	75g	0.11
Vegetables			Dandelion leaves	75g	0.1
Soya beans	100g	1.03	Chickpeas	100g	0.004
Brussels sprouts	100g	0.26			
Cauliflower	100g	0.21			
Broccoli	100g	0.2			
Cabbage	75g	0.17			
Kale	75g	0.13			
Green beans	75g	0.11			
Spinach	200g	0.1			

quick tips to get
more omega 3

As you can see, there's a wide choice of foods that will enable you to top up your omega 3 fatty acids simply by swapping ingredients or adding ordinary everyday foods to your diet.

Try to eat a wide variety of oily fish and seafood, so that you can benefit from all their other good nutrients. Tuna is a good source of omega 3 fatty acids, but the tinning process reduces the amount so that it doesn't count as a portion of oily fish. Tinned sardines and mackerel do though. Although these oily fish and seafood are by far the richest sources of the essential

fatty acids, there are many plant foods that also contribute useful quantities. Some of them, like nuts, seeds and oils, are good sources, so make sure you use them regularly as replacements for your normal oils, nibbles and garnishes.

Although aiming for 1g of omega 3s a day is the optimal target, getting half a gram (500mg) is an excellent healthy baseline – and it's at least twice as much as most people consume. Adding some cloves or oregano to a recipe, putting some tofu into any stew or casserole, mixing flax seed and walnut oil into your salad dressings, sprinkling pine nuts on your yogurt, chopped walnuts on a salad or adding sesame seeds to your home-made bread will all make a significant and valuable contribution to your total omega 3 consumption.

Instead of salted peanuts, use chopped walnuts, pistachios and pumpkin seeds as a nibble to go with a drink or to munch while you watch TV in the evening to boost your omega 3 intake.

It's almost impossible to go short of the basic omega 6 fatty acids – and, as we've seen before, it's an excess of these in relation to the omega 3s that can have an adverse effect on your health. Switching to rapeseed (canola) oil for your cooking and frying is an extremely important step as not only will this give you a substantial increase in omega 3s, but this oil has the very best ratio of 3s to 6s. As it has a high smoking point, food cooks much more quickly, sealing the outside and reducing the amount of fats absorbed by the food. This is a good thing as most people in the Western world consume far too much fat – and whether it's good or bad fat, it still contains extremely high number of calories. If you must eat fried food, the small loss of omega 3s is more than offset by the gains through less total fat and a reduced amount of omega 6.

what if I am a vegetarian or vegan?

Oily fish – like mackerel, herring, sardines and tuna – are the only source of EPA omega 3, so if you don't like eating fish take a fish oil supplement.

If you're vegetarian or vegan you can get tiny amounts of EPA from flax-seed oil or purslane (a green, leafy veg) because your body can convert some of the omega 3s into EPA but it's very little and a very inefficient conversion process. As you can see from the charts and recipes in this book, the alpha-linolenic acid (ALA) can be found in some green leafy vegetables and some nuts and seeds and their oils, especially flax seeds, flax-seed oil, pumpkin seeds, walnuts, walnut oil and rapeseed (canola) oil. It's this ALA the body must convert into EPA, the omega 3 found in substantial quantities in all oily fish as well as shellfish, seafood and some white fish.

In spite of the assertions of the vegetarian and vegan groups, not all people can make this conversion at all (young children and men especially struggle), and for those who can it's an extremely inefficient process that results in tiny amounts of EPA which are certainly not enough to supply all the body's requirements. To make matters worse, it appears that the whole process becomes less efficient with age.

To illustrate this point, studies have shown that the amount of DHA omega 3s in the body tissues of vegetarians is only half of that found in meat and fish eaters. Bearing in mind that the average body levels of DHA fall far short of our optimum requirements, I find this very worrying.

The EFAs from fish are a major issue for both veggies and vegans and very few are prepared to compromise over the question of fish oil supplements. To me, this is a serious concern, especially for women of child-bearing age and young children. For proper growth, function and development of the brain and central nervous system, some omega 3s from fish and omega 6s from meat and dairy products are vital. None of these are available from a totally vegan or vegetarian diet and claims that the body can make all it needs from plant oils like flax seed are poorly substantiated. While I would defend absolutely anyone's right to personal choice, I do worry about the morality of putting the health of a baby, infant or child at risk just to satisfy the beliefs of the parents.

If non-fish eaters won't take fish supplements, they should take high-strength flax-seed oil supplements and include substantial amounts of the vegetables, nuts, seeds and oils that provide the greatest concentration of the non-fish derived omega 3 ALA.

The body also requires the appropriate constituents of the omega 6 family. But keeping the ideal balance of omega 3 to 6 means choosing carefully in order not to push up the omega 6 levels to those universally found in most people's diets. The worst culprits are commercial vegetable oils, like corn, sunflower and peanut oils. By far the healthiest oil for cooking, with the best omega 3 to 6 ratio, is rapeseed (canola). But even better for general food use, which doesn't involve high temperature cooking, is flax-seed oil, which is easily top of the vegetable oil table thanks to its high content of omega 3.

Use it generously on salads, pasta, cooked vegetables, soups and smoothies. Wherever possible, choose cold pressed organic varieties for maximum benefit. Another very rich source are flax seeds themselves and, when ground, they make an ideal sprinkle for porridge, breakfast cereals, cooked fruits, crumbles, salads and can be added to bread and cake mixtures.

But note that both flax seeds and their oil are easily oxidised, which means that they will go rancid, making them unpalatable and unhealthy as the protective fats become damaging free radicals. Only buy oil stored in dark bottles or seeds in dark tubs and keep in the fridge. Flax-seed oil should be stored in shops in the chill cabinet and, like the seeds, should have a short sell-by date of 6 months to a year.

To maximise the conversion process, it is also important to make sure that your diet is not deficient in other nutrients. Vitamins B and C as well as zinc and magnesium will help you convert plant sources. Avoid unhealthy fats and make sure that you lead a healthy lifestyle with as little stress as possible.

Another nutrient highly likely to be missing in the vegetarian diet is vitamin D. There are small amounts of vitamin D in dairy products, although oily fish is the richest source. The body is able to manufacture this vitamin – essential for absorbing calcium – when ultra-violet light from the sun reaches the skin. But unfortunately, in the UK the necessary wave-lengths are only present during the summer months – if we're lucky.

The simple vegetarian diet

Stick to the rule of 'thirds' and you can't go wrong. Just plan your day's food to be one-third fresh produce (fruit, vegetables and salads), one-third starchy foods (wholemeal bread, wholegrain cereals, pasta, rice) and the final third of beans, soya products, nuts, seeds, cheese, milk, yogurt and eggs. Then add a 10 per cent bonus. That can be cream, chocolate, a gooey dessert, a piece of cake or your favourite ice cream.

Just make sure that each meal contains the same proportion of foods in each section and you'll have a perfectly balanced diet as long as you vary your choices every day.

Demi-vegetarians

The phrase 'demi-veg' is growing more popular and it generally means people who've given up all red meat, but who will eat the occasional chicken or fish. Naturally this makes balancing the daily menus easier as a lot of the protein, iron and vitamin D and EFA requirements are taken care of.

'smart food'

What about functional foods?

As the importance of all the omega fats becomes more evident, food manufacturers and processors are trampling each other in the stampede to get their functional food products onto the supermarket shelves. Juices, yogurts, cereal bars, fruit bars, breakfast cereals, spreads and even eggs are being enriched with the essential fats.

Don't be fooled though. Most of them have added plant-derived omega 3s and usually in quantities that provide little benefit. Even the ones which have added fish oils tend to use fairly insignificant amounts – and most of those I've tasted would be unacceptable, especially to the children at whom many of these are targeted. It's also worrying that they don't declare the sources of these extra ingredients – and it's the fish oils that concern me most as all but the most expensive carry the risk of contamination with heavy metals and toxic chemical residues.

Organic milk

In an ideal world, we would all choose to eat organically, but cost and availability make this almost impossible for most people. I'm certain that the vital area, particularly for young families and women who are trying to become pregnant, who are pregnant, breast feeding or bringing up young children, is the whole range of dairy products.

If you could afford nothing else, buy as much organic milk, yogurt, cheese, butter and eggs as you possibly can. There's no doubt that they're safer as they won't contain hormones, antibiotics and chemical residues from insecticides, herbicides and fungicides – which are all potentially toxic for the foetus, baby, infant and toddler. Added to which, they're no great gift to adults, either.

On the plus side, organic milk is a nutritionally better choice as it contains more of the plant sources of omega 3 fatty acids than conventional milk (because the animals are reared on grass). While these aren't as beneficial as the EPA and DHA from oily fish, they will add to the base level of omega 3s in the body and therefore increase the amount converted into the long chain fats. As we've already seen, this is not an efficient process – which makes it all the more important for vegetarians to increase their consumption of plant sources. This benefit follows through from milk to all its derivatives.

> My advice would always be to concentrate on natural sources of omega 3 and only use these more expensive, but less beneficial functional foods as a top-up.

supplements

Although in theory it's always best to get your life-supporting and health-protective nutrients from the food you eat, this is not always a practical proposition. We should all be eating oily fish but many children don't like fish, vegetarians and vegans don't eat fish, fish allergies are quite common, sometimes other medical problems make it difficult to chew or swallow normal food and dare I say it, there are even adults who won't eat fish.

In these situations supplements are essential and there are also times when those who eat fish may need a boost of their essential fatty acids when it is just not possible to get them from food alone. The prime example of how supplements can be of benefit is the work done by Dr Alex Richardson at Oxford University. She is one of the world's authorities on the link between behaviour and mental function and a deficiency of essential fatty acids. She's been the lead researcher in many studies including those carried out with school children here in the UK. Nevertheless, do remember though that supplements are just that – a way of supplementing the body's intake of specific nutrients – they can never be a substitute for food.

If you're dealing with problem children who have ADHD, dyslexia or dyspraxia, the last thing any parent wants is a prescription for behaviour-modifying drugs. Since essential fatty acids can help a significant proportion of these youngsters, it seems to me that this must be the first place to start. When you do start using any supplements, whether it's for adults or children, the first thing to do is make sure they're of the best-possible quality. Many people believe that price is the key therefore the most expensive must be the best but this is absolutely not the case. Conversely the very cheapest may turn out to be poor quality and contain very small doses so a packet that looks cheap on the shelf doesn't last long if you need to take nine capsules a day to get a sensible amount of EFAs.

How to choose your supplement

When looking at fish oil supplements you must be satisfied that:

● the manufacturer gets their oil from fish in the least-polluted waters.
● they use the most up-to-date technology to clean and remove potential contaminants from the oil.
● whether oil or capsules, the products are in dark-coloured glass or light-proof boxes and that in the shop they're nowhere near a heat source or very bright lights. I think the oil remedies are best kept refrigerated.
● check expiry dates and don't buy if they're getting pretty close – look at the bottles or packets right at the back of the shelf, they usually have longer sell-by dates as they're the newest stock.
● if you're using flax-seed oils I would always insist on organic products in light-proof packaging and refrigeration in store.
● ground flax seeds oxidise and go rancid very quickly so these too should be in air-proof, light-proof containers with at least six months before the expiry date.
● read the labels carefully. If you're shopping for a child with ADHD the last thing you want is any artificial colourings, flavourings, preservatives or fillers, and you'd be amazed by how many companies fill their pills with junk.
● check the dose per capsule. The best manufacturer I know provides 500mg in two capsules which is a daily dose. The worst has 25mg per capsule which means taking 10 in the morning and 10 in the evening – try that with a child. Although the best look much more expensive, they actually work out at costing less per day than the cheapest.
● the advice of Dr Alex Richardson on relative content of EPA and DHA is very important. Her evidence suggests that high EPA supplements are the most effective for ADHD, dyslexia and dyspraxia but during pregnancy and breastfeeding a high DHA is needed as this is the fatty acid used to make brain cells.

Fish oil and fish liver oil

Since the beginning of the last century the Hull trawlermen knew that cod liver oil helped with the stiffness, aches, angina and arthritis that went with the intensive labour and awful weather conditions for sea-going fishermen. It's for these anti-inflammatory benefits that cod liver oil is most effective – a fact that has been well established by research carried out at Cardiff University by the world-renowned Professor Bruce Caterson and his colleagues. It's even more essential to make sure that cod liver oil has been thoroughly purified as the fish's liver is where heavy metals and toxic chemicals are most likely to accumulate.

It's also important to watch out for the high vitamin A content of all fish liver oils, so don't exceed the recommended dose and don't take other vitamin supplements containing vitamin A at the same time as fish liver oils (as vitamin A can be harmful in large quantities). These should always be avoided during pregnancy because of the vitamin A but fish oil supplements are a good thing to take before, during and after pregnancy.

getting the best from essential fatty acids

Although it might seem that the essential fatty acids are the answer to many of life's health problems, they do not work in isolation. Whether you choose to eat all the special foods in this book, take supplements or have a mixture of the two, unless your overall nutrition is up to scratch, there is no way your body will be able to maximise the full benefits of these amazing nutrients.

Patently, average consumers – men, women and children – in the UK, America and much of northern Europe are failing to do that. Healthy eating means getting enough of all the essential nutrients from a diet which is rich in variety and poor in the damaging saturated fats, refined carbohydrates, sugar, salt and junk foods. All the available evidence shows that in Great Britain:

- 95 per cent of adults are deficient in folic acid.
- 60 per cent of women are short of iron.
- 90 per cent of men and women miss out on vitamin B6.
- 50 per cent of women fall short of the daily requirement of vitamin A.
- 50 per cent of children don't get enough vitamins A, B12, D, E and folic acid.
- many adults and children go short of calcium, iron, selenium and zinc.
- 20 per cent of 4–18-year-olds eat no fruit.

Type 2 (Non-Insulin Dependent diabetes or NIDD) now affects young children, because . . .
- 20 per cent of children are now clinically obese.
- the vast majority do not come near to the optimum amount of EFAs.
- the vast majority consume far too much omega 6.

These figures are proof that, as a nation, we are not getting it right in terms of diet. You only have to look at the facts. The French have less heart disease. Greek men live longer. Japanese women have less breast cancer and osteoporosis. All because their diets are much richer in the best EFAs and all the antioxidant protective foods with the highest ORAC scores (see page 31). So because our average diet is poor it's hardly surprising that adding EFAs is going to improve a variety of health problems.

ADHD, dyslexia and associated problems

There are now many controlled trials which show the benefits of omega 3 fatty acids in the treatment of ADHD, dyslexia and other learning and behavioural difficulties. These are not all randomised, double-blind studies, but the number of children involved, the dramatic change in those with severe problems, plus the significant improvement in academic performance in children without problems is, from my point of view, evidence enough. Having used fish oil supplements and dietary changes in the treatment of these troubled children for more than 20 years, I'm convinced that around a third of these youngsters will benefit. The fact that there is absolutely no risk in making these simple changes, plus the fact that the essential fatty acids play a key role in overall health, should be more than enough to justify this regime as the first treatment of choice rather than the ever-growing prescription of Ritalin and its relatives. One of the world's leading authorities, Dr Alex Richardson of Oxford University, has not only carried out her own studies, but also runs a website describing all published research and giving the latest news updates on this topic – see www.fabresearch.org

Preventing and treating heart disease

There is a wealth of evidence that supports the beneficial properties of omega 3 fatty acids as a group of nutrients that are beneficial in the prevention and treatment of heart disease. A recent review of the data has found that people encouraged to increase their total fish consumption including oily fish was strongly associated with an overall reduction in death from all causes. Another study published in 2003 also found that patients consuming regular and significant amounts of all fish benefited from a relative risk reduction in all causes of mortality of at least 50 per cent when compared with patients who habitually did not eat fish.

Because heart specialists in the UK are worried that fish oils are not routinely prescribed to their patients the National Institute for Health and Clinical Excellence (NICE) is currently developing practice guidelines for the NHS prescription of fish oil supplements to help prevent secondary heart attacks after an initial episode. Their recommendation published in their Consultation Draft is 1g of fish oil every day for those surviving heart attacks and they further advise following a Mediterranean-type diet which includes 2–4 weekly portions of oily fish.

There's further support for this evidence from the British Heart Foundation, which advises everyone at risk of cardiovascular disease to increase the amount of oily fish in their diets or consider supplements. The American Heart Association recommends fish oil supplements as one of the important self-help steps for heart health.

Arthritis

Fish don't get arthritis. The EPA and DHA in fish oils are powerful anti-inflammatories and this is particularly effective in their ability to control the inflammatory process that occurs at joint surfaces damaged by disease or injury. So much so that as little as a teaspoon a day or one good portion of herring, mackerel or sardines can relieve joint pain in rheumatoid and osteoarthritis. The effect is so marked that morning stiffness and daily pain improve enough for patients to stop most or sometimes all of their conventional anti-inflammatory drugs.

Asthma and other allergies

Because of their anti-inflammatory qualities omega 3 fatty acids can help reduce asthma and other allergies too.

Chronic fatigue syndrome and M.E.

Over the years, I've used a combination of fish oil supplements, zinc and selenium combined with diet and graded exercise to help patients with these conditions. The responses vary and this regime doesn't help all sufferers. But a significant number improve dramatically. Professor Basant Puri at London's Hammersmith Hospital has been working with this group of patients for years and describes in his book *Chronic Fatigue Syndrome* his successful use of omega 3 and omega 6 fatty acids.

A good mood food

Dr Sarah Conkin from the University Of Pittsburgh School of Medicine says that eating salmon and other high omega 3 foods could help you feel better whether you're in a bad mood or suffering from depression. Using standard psychological tests, she found that people with high levels of omega 3s in their blood were generally happier and more agreeable than those in her study with low levels of fatty acids, who were more likely to suffer mild to moderate depression, impulsive behaviour and moodiness.

For skin protection and healing

Dry, scaly skin patches, eczema and, to a lesser extent, psoriasis, dandruff, lifeless hair and flaking nails are all problems that may be a sign of deficiency but will almost certainly be improved by getting more from your diet and taking supplements. Of course, it's important to make sure that there's no question of fish allergies, especially when giving fish oil supplements to small children. Researchers at Manchester University have recently found that omega 3s in the diet or taken as supplements, can help increase the skin's tolerance of sunburn. But that's not an excuse to skip the high-factor sun cream.

Good vision

There's no doubt that eating oily fish helps to maintain good eyesight – omega 3 deficiencies may show up as blurring, glare, sensitivity to light, poor night vision and eye strain.

Dry-eye syndrome

This is a very distressing problem, which causes great discomfort and often leads to infections. It can be related to some of the less common arthritic diseases, but other than using artificial tear drops, there's little in the way of treatment. However, high-dose fish oil supplements have been found to be a considerable help for some patients.

Old age

Our bodies need omega 3 as they're the starting point for the production of a number of substances that control vital bodily functions. As we've seen earlier in this book, the body needs these nutrients for the growth and development of the brain and central nervous system – and they're just as important at the other end of the age spectrum. They appear to give some protection against developing Alzheimer's disease and, in supplement form, to slow its progression in the early stages of the illness.

The only healthy diet is a varied one

From pre-conception to death, essential fatty acids are one of the most important groups of nutrients. A lifetime consumption of regular amounts of oily fish and the use of supplements when necessary is a major building block for good health.

But no single vitamin, mineral or supplement is the key to a long and healthy life. To maximise the benefits of essential fatty acids you need appropriate amounts of other fats, proteins, good carbohydrates, vitamins and minerals. What few people realise is the enormous importance of nature's protective antioxidants in the battle for good health and survival against the damaging free radicals.

Antioxidants are highly protective natural components found throughout nature and often at the highest concentrations in brightly coloured fruits and vegetables. In their natural state, plants contain more than 4,000 of these vital substances, which protect against many life-threatening conditions like heart disease, arterial damage and many forms of cancer. This is why your five daily portions of fruit and veg are so important. Many American experts even say everyone should aim for seven portions a day – and I'm certain they're right.

Scientists at the US Department of Agriculture, Human Nutrition Research Center on Aging at Tufts University developed a new method of testing the antioxidant effect of foods. It measures the oxygen radical absorbance capacity (ORAC) – the ability of a food to absorb and neutralise cell-damaging free radicals – and researchers produced a league table of high ORAC food.

They calculate that 3,000 ORAC units a day is what the average person needs for good protection, but if you push it up to 5,000 ORACs you're in the super protective bracket. I'm ashamed to tell you that in the UK most people struggle to reach 1,500 ORACs. But it's so easy – 100g of prunes, for example, has 5,570 ORACs, you get more than 2,000 from a small punnet of blueberries or blackberries and the same from a decent portion of strawberries, raspberries, curly kale or red cabbage. A portion of Brussels sprouts, broccoli, beetroot, oranges, black grapes, red peppers, plums, cherries, avocado or kiwi provides around 1,000 units. A bit of planning when you shop and common sense when you eat is all you need. Don't forget that you can count a glass of fruit or vegetable juice or a vegetarian pizza as one portion; they'll both give you high ORAC scores.

If you divide your daily food into one-third fresh fruit and veg, one-third complex carbohydrates like wholegrain cereals, beans, pasta, brown rice, oats, good wholemeal bread, potatoes (but not all chips), one-sixth protein (meat, fish, eggs, beans) one-sixth

dairy products and an extra 10 per cent for treats like cream, chocolates, cakes, biscuits and alcohol, you won't go far wrong. Build your daily food around the recipes in this book, take supplements to boost your levels whenever necessary and make sure you eat a varied and balanced diet if you want to improve your health, prevent disease and enhance your intellectual performance.

smart recipes

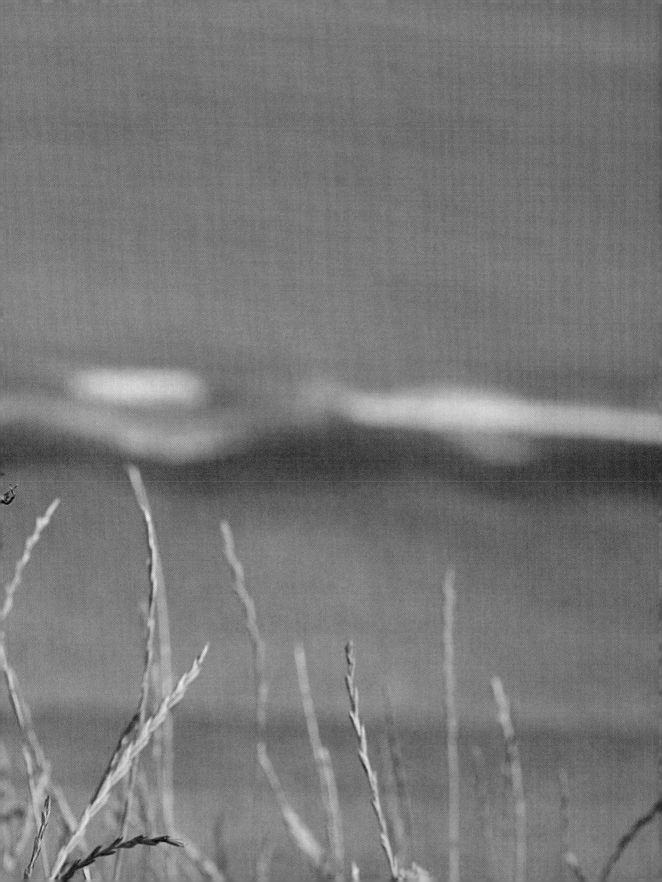

breakfasts

buckwheaties

strawberry sundae crunch

Buckwheat isn't a real cereal. In fact, the plant is related to rhubarb. It's extremely rich in a natural chemical called rutin, which keeps the inner lining of blood vessels clear and healthy and helps prevent chilblains and broken veins. As well as EFAs, the sesame seeds provide vitamin E, essential for sexual function, and you also get a circulation boost from the cinnamon and calcium from the milk.

Makes 10–12

225g buckwheat flour
1 egg, beaten
1 tablespoon brown caster sugar
2 teaspoons ground cinnamon
About 300ml semi-skimmed milk
75g unsalted butter
4 large dessert apples, cored and cut into rings
2 tablespoons sesame seeds

Combine the flour, egg, sugar and cinnamon in a bowl and mix with enough milk to make a smooth batter.

Heat the butter gently in a frying pan. Dip the apple rings in the batter, then sauté in the butter until crisp. You may need to do this in batches.

Serve with the sesame seeds scattered on top.

Mixing cheese, strawberries and cereals may seem a bit odd. But believe me, it works. Cottage cheese is a good source of calcium and protein. The cereal gives you lots of high-fibre and low-GI carbohydrates. And the orange juice and salad, of course, add a good dose of vitamin C. The toasted flax seeds are a rich source of essential fatty acids.

Serves 2

225g strawberries, hulled
200ml freshly squeezed orange juice
2 teaspoons brown caster sugar
250g cottage cheese
2 tablespoons flax seeds
75g sugar-free organic muesli
1 large handful mixed salad leaves
2 teaspoons orange zest

Put half the strawberries, 2 tablespoons of the orange juice and the sugar into a blender or food processor and whizz until smooth.

Mix the cottage cheese with the rest of the orange juice, flax seeds and muesli. Divide between 2 small bowls. Arrange the salad leaves on the side.

Slice the remaining strawberries and add to the salad. Pour the liquidised sauce over and sprinkle with the orange zest.

mountain muesli

Tipping cheap muesli into a bowl and adding milk is like eating sawdust. But when you have the real thing, as enjoyed by mountain herdsmen in the Swiss Alps, your breakfast will take you comfortably to lunchtime without a mid-morning energy dip. As well as protein, energy and vitamins from the oats, more instant energy from the dried fruits, and a healthy dose of fibre, you will get some essential fatty acids from the mixture of nuts and an added boost from the ground flax seeds.

Allow a serving bowl per person

Organic muesli
Apple, orange or pineapple juice
Plain live yogurt
Runny honey
Fresh fruit – apple, pear, banana or soft fruit in season
Ground flax seeds

Proper muesli is prepared the night before in individual bowls and left in the fridge. For each serving of muesli, stir in enough fruit juice to moisten it well, a tablespoonful of yogurt, and a teaspoonful of honey.

In the morning, take it out of the fridge as early as possible, and just before eating, stir in the fruit of your choice – grated apple or pear, sliced banana, a few strawberries, a sliced peach and a couple of teaspoons of the flax seed. At the Bircher-Benner Clinic in Switzerland, where muesli originated, they add fresh blackberries and some thick cream.

kale, tofu and potato pancakes

My wife is half Irish and remembers a variation of these from her childhood, as potatoes are a traditional part of the Irish diet. We make these pancakes with kale or other dark green vegetables from our garden – including Brussels sprout tops or rocket which has survived the winter. They're delicious and provide cancer-protective nutrients, folic acid, fibre, lots of vitamin C and, because we use tofu instead of the traditional bacon, there's the added bonus of more EFAs and less saturated fat.

Serves 4

For the pancakes:
450g potatoes, peeled and diced
60g plain flour
About 200ml milk

For the filling:
60g unsalted butter
225g diced tofu
450g kale, finely shredded

Put the potatoes and flour in a blender or food processor and whizz with enough milk to make a batter. Let the batter rest for 30 minutes.

Meanwhile, heat 20g of the butter in a pan and fry the tofu for 2 minutes. Add the kale and a few tablespoons of cold water, cook for 5 minutes and drain.

Heat the rest of the butter in a small non-stick frying pan. Add a small ladle of batter to make a thin pancake and cook until golden. Add a quarter of the filling, fold the pancake over and serve. Repeat with the rest of the ingredients.

porridge and kipper soup

I was on holiday on the Isle of Skye when I first saw this dish offered on a menu. Quite honestly, I thought it sounded disgusting. I was persuaded to try it, however, and it tasted wonderful. Whenever we make it at home, it always brings back memories of heather-covered hillsides and the mist coming in over the Irish Sea. It is rich in mood-soothing ingredients in the oats, a good balance of omega 3 and 6 fatty acids from the kipper and protective plant chemicals from the garlic, leeks and onions.

Serves 2–3

2 tablespoons olive oil
50g unsalted butter
2 large onions, finely chopped
2 leeks, washed and finely chopped
1 garlic clove, finely chopped
1 floury potato, peeled and grated
1 fat carrot, grated
4 skinned kipper fillets
80g fine porridge oats
2 generous tablespoons double cream
1 tablespoon flax seeds

Heat the oil and half the butter in a pan and sweat the onions, leeks, garlic, potato and carrot for 15 minutes. Pour in 850ml water and simmer for a further 15 minutes.

Meanwhile, bring a separate pan of water to the boil, add the remaining butter and poach the kipper fillets for 6 minutes. Drain the fish, then flake them and add to the soup along with the porridge oats. Leave to stand, covered, for at least 10 minutes. Divide the soup between serving bowls and top with a dollop of cream and a sprinkling of flax seeds.

kipper in a jug

Kippers, like all smoked fish, can contain a lot of salt. This cooking method removes a lot of it, leaves other vital nutrients intact and avoids all the problems of cooking smells usually associated with this delicious fish. Kippers are an exceptionally rich source of essential fatty acids and vitamin D.

Whether you're suffering from winter aches and pains or summer hay fever, essential fatty acids are effective anti-inflammatories and will help relieve the symptoms. You also get lots of calcium, zinc, selenium, massive doses of vitamins D, B12, biotin and niacin.

Serves as many as you like

1 undyed kipper per person
Boiling water, to cover
Wholemeal bread and butter, to serve

Get a jug large enough to hold the kipper without the tail sticking out of the top. Add the boiling water and cover tightly with kitchen foil. Leave for 6 minutes.

Remove the fish and serve with a small knob of butter and wholemeal bread.

tijuana hash

This is a spicy version of traditional hash brown potatoes, far removed from the anaemic, tasteless ready-made versions so often served in English hotels and cafés. A great breakfast, brunch, lunch or supper dish and you can make a mountain of it in half an hour. It's filling and sustaining and is an unusual source of essential fatty acids from the spices and pistachio nuts. You can add a bit more, and some protein, by topping each portion with a couple of fried eggs.

Serves 4

500g old potatoes, peeled and diced
½ teaspoon paprika
½ teaspoon ground cumin
½ teaspoon chilli powder
½ teaspoon ground cloves
Pinch of turmeric
½ red onion, grated
100g pancetta, finely cubed
100g Gruyère cheese, grated
1 tablespoon olive oil
100g shelled unsalted pistachios

Preheat the grill to high.

Boil the potatoes until just soft – about 10 minutes. Drain, put into a bowl and sprinkle with the spices. Add the grated onion and crush lightly with a wooden spoon.

Heat the oil on medium heat in an ovenproof frying pan and cook the pancetta until crisp. Add the potato mixture and pistachios to the pan and cook gently for 5–6 minutes, turning once or twice. Flatten the mixture to fill the pan and when the bottom begins browning, add the cheese and put under the grill until the top is brown and bubbling.

a bone-building breakfast

Tinned sardines are wonderful. They're inexpensive, instant and absolutely dripping with good nutrition. But to get the best out of these fabulous little fish there are a couple of things you need to know. Ideally buy them tinned in extra virgin olive oil, or rapeseed (canola) oil as the next best option. Do not buy them in 'vegetable oil', corn or sunflower oil which will give you too much omega 6 and not enough omega 3, or tomato sauce. Never remove the bones as they're a terrific source of well-absorbed natural calcium – they're already cooked and very soft; just mash them with a fork. Strong bones, heart protection, cancer protection and anti-inflammatory constituents that are good for the skin, lungs and even the pain of arthritis – what more could you ask for first thing in the morning?

Serves 1

120g tin sardines in extra virgin olive oil
2 teaspoons tomato ketchup
2 teaspoons low-fat mayonnaise
Few drops Worcester sauce, to taste
Freshly ground black pepper
2 slices coarse wholemeal toast
1 tomato, quartered

Preheat the grill to medium-high.

Thoroughly mash the sardines, ketchup, mayo, Worcester sauce and pepper with a fork until the bones are all smashed and you have a thick creamy consistency.

Divide the mixture between the 2 slices of toast. Put them on a sheet of foil under the grill until the fish starts to brown – about 3 minutes. Remove and serve at once with the tomato.

athole brose

This is a variation on another traditional dish I first had during a wonderful holiday in Scotland. My wife thought I was crazy to have uncooked porridge and whisky at breakfast time – especially as I hardly drink at all. But believe me, it was delicious – just what I needed to set me up for a stimulating morning's walking. Slow-release energy, instant get-up-and-go and a healthy shot of omega 3s to go with the whisky.

Serves 2

100g raspberries
1 tablespoon lemon juice
1 teaspoon brown caster sugar
150ml whipping cream
2 tablespoons runny honey
2 tablespoons single-malt whisky
25g porridge oats
2 heaped tablespoons crushed walnuts

Heat half the raspberries with the lemon juice and sugar in a small pan for 2 minutes. Set aside to cool.

Whip the cream with the honey. Beat in the whisky. Fold in the porridge oats. Put the raspberry sauce into 2 bowls and spoon the porridge mixture over. Serve with the remaining raspberries and crushed walnuts on top.

an irish breakfast

There are as many recipes for colcannon as there are Irish daughters, mothers and grandmothers but this is my favourite. We all know how important it is to eat our greens because of the protective nutrients they contain, but few people understand that all of the cabbage family are good for the eyes, heart, cancer protection and contain useful amounts of essential fatty acids.

Serves 6

1kg old potatoes, preferably Desirée, peeled and diced
700g kale, finely shredded
Pinch of coarse sea salt
300ml semi-skimmed milk
2 spring onions, finely chopped
2 tablespoons double cream
50g unsalted butter
6 free-range organic eggs
Freshly ground black pepper

Steam the potatoes until just cooked (about 20 minutes). Sprinkle the kale with a pinch or two of sea salt and steam until tender (about 10 minutes). Put the milk and spring onions in a pan and bring almost to the boil. Mash the potatoes adding a little hot milk and spring onion mixture at a time until it is really smooth. Add the cream, and whisk with a fork. Add the kale, some black pepper and mix thoroughly together. Turn into a hot dish.

Poach the eggs (see my tip on page 68). Put a mound of colcannon onto each plate. Make a hollow in the top, add a knob of butter and a poached egg without breaking the yolk. Sticking your fork in the egg and watching the deep yellow yolk of an organic egg trickle over the potato is half the fun. Serve with a few twists of black pepper.

sprouts with black pudding, apple and bacon

This is a quick, simple and tasty snack which you can eat any time at home using fresh or frozen sprouts. It's perfect as a supper dish though is just as good as a winter afternoon treat sitting round the fire. It combines some of the best of English ingredients with the bacon, black pudding and apple. Because it's free-range, all organic meat contains heart-protective CLA (conjugated linoleic acid) and some essential fatty acids. You'll get a bit extra from the rapeseed oil.

Serves 2

8 Brussels sprouts, halved
2 teaspoons rapeseed oil
8 slices black pudding
4 rashers organic English back bacon
1 large Cox's apple
2 teaspoons butter
2 thick slices toasted brioche

Steam the Brussels sprouts for about 5 minutes. Meanwhile heat the oil in a large pan, and add the black pudding and bacon. Cook for about 10 minutes, turning, and add the steamed sprouts to the pan.

Quarter the apple, remove the core and cut each quarter in 2 slices. Melt the butter in a small frying pan, add the apple slices and cook over a low heat for 2–3 minutes until they start to soften.

Put 1 slice of the toasted brioche onto each of 2 warmed plates. Put 2 rashers of bacon on each slice, topped with 4 slices of black pudding. Arrange the sprouts on one side of the plate and the sautéed apple on the other and enjoy.

denzil's welsh rarebit

Welsh rarebit always reminds me of Sunday tea – when it was simply a slice of bread and cheese stuck under the grill until it bubbled. But this dish, given to me by my Welsh neighbour makes more of a meal for Sunday breakfast. As we all know, cheese and apples make perfect partners, but here both are cooked and have the added flavour, EFAs, calcium and protein benefit of smoked tofu.

Serves 2

2 slices thick wholemeal bread
175g red Leicester cheese, grated
2 shakes of Worcester sauce – more if you like your
    food spicy
1 teaspoon mustard powder
25ml semi-skimmed milk
Freshly ground black pepper
150g cubes smoked tofu
50g unsalted butter
1 large red apple, cored but not peeled, cut into 8 wedges
2 free-range eggs, preferably organic

Heat the grill – a toaster won't do – and toast the bread on one side. Mix together the cheese, Worcester sauce, mustard powder, milk and pepper to form a smooth paste. Crumble in the tofu. Spread this mixture on the untoasted side of the bread.

Melt the butter in a small frying pan, add the apple wedges and cook over a medium heat, turning as necessary.

While the apples are cooking, put the eggs on to poach and put the bread and cheese back under the grill, cheese-side up. When they're golden and bubbling, remove to the centre of 2 warm plates. Serve with the apples on one side and the eggs on top.

sardine cheese bake

This robust breakfast is ideal for those lazy Sunday mornings when you get up late and don't plan to eat again until the evening. It's packed with flavour and goodness and works well with fresh fillets of any oily fish – mackerel, herrings or pilchards, for example. And the spinach adds yet more points to your omega 3 daily score. Protein, iron, zinc, essential fatty acids and vitamin D are provided by the sardines, and with folic acid from the spinach, complex carbohydrates from the rice and calcium from the cheese this makes the ideal start to a day of physical exertion.

Serves 4

2 medium eggs, preferably organic
50g rice, cooked
125g Cheddar cheese
350g sardine fillets, skinned
700g baby spinach

Preheat the oven to 200°C/400°F/gas mark 6.

Beat the eggs and mix together with half the rice and half the cheese. Put half the mixture into an oven-proof dish and place the fish on top.

Cover with rest of the rice mixture. Scatter the remaining cheese on top and cook for 35 minutes.

When the bake is almost ready, steam the spinach (very lightly, for about 2 minutes). Serve the bake on a bed of spinach.

cod roe with poached eggs

Cod roe is a wonderful source of vitamin D, and this recipe provides more than twice your day's requirements in one portion. It's not always easy to find but is worth seeking out – chat up your fishmonger! This is quick, simple and full of essential fatty acids and other nutrients.

Serves 4

700g cod roe
2 organic eggs, whisked
6 tablespoons plain flour
3 tablespoons rapeseed oil
1 large handful each of rocket and watercress,
   thoroughly washed
4 poached eggs
Wholegrain bread, toasted, to serve

Slice the cod roe into 1cm slices. Dip them in the egg, then the flour. Heat the oil gently in a pan, then add the cod roe slices, cooking for 2–3 minutes on each side.

Put a pile of mixed rocket and watercress on each plate. Place the cod roe slices on top, then the poached eggs. Serve with triangles of toasted bread.

soups and starters

spinach with yogurt

This soup, from Crete, includes those Greek favourites, spinach and yogurt, with added paprika and flax-seed oil. The combination of spinach and flax-seed oil produces a significant portion of essential fatty acids – a whole week's worth in fact.

Serves 4

20ml flax-seed oil
25g unsalted butter
1 large garlic clove, very finely chopped
225g baby spinach
1 tablespoon fresh mint, finely chopped
1kg sheep's milk yogurt
1 teaspoon crushed caraway seeds
Pinch of paprika
4 small mint sprigs, to garnish

Put the oil and butter into a large saucepan. Add the garlic and sauté gently for 2 minutes. Wash the spinach thoroughly and add to the pan with only the water still clinging to it. Add the mint. Cover and steam slowly, shaking the pan every 30 seconds or so, until the spinach is wilted – about 5 minutes.

Put the yogurt into another pan with the caraway seeds. Heat through, but don't boil. Add the spinach and its juices and stir well. Serve sprinkled sparingly with paprika and decorated with mint sprigs.

bean and pasta soup

This is an EFA-rich adaptation of the Italian peasant soup, *pasta e fagioli,* closer to the Naples version than the butter and pancetta recipe that you'll find in the rest of Italy. It provides protein and heart-protective natural chemicals in the beans, and an amazing content of beta-carotene and other vital carotenoids in the chard. Chard and beans are also valuable sources of omega 3s.

Serves 6–8

5 tablespoons olive oil
1 small onion, finely chopped
2 garlic cloves, finely chopped
1 carrot, finely diced
1 stick celery, finely sliced
225g chard, leaves stripped from the stalks
1.8 litres vegetable stock, preferably home-made or use a good low-salt cube or bouillon powder such as Kallo or Marigold
350g (drained weight) tinned cannellini, butter beans or other white beans, drained and well rinsed
250g small pasta such as fusilli or farfalle – or farfel, small grain-like pieces of toasted pasta
6 tablespoons freshly grated Parmesan cheese mixed with 2 tablespoons ground flax seeds

Put the oil into a large pan and gently sauté the onion, garlic, carrot, celery and chard stalks for about 10 minutes. Add the stock and bring to a boil. Add the beans to the soup and bring back to a boil. After 2 minutes, add the torn green chard leaves and cook for another 3–4 minutes until the beans are tender. Keep warm.

Cook the pasta according to packet instructions. Drain and add to the bean mixture. Serve with the Parmesan and flax seed mixture sprinkled on each bowl.

leftover soup with dolcelatte

One of my earliest food revelations was Brussels sprout and Stilton soup, which I tasted on Boxing Day after spending Christmas with a schoolfriend and his family, when I was about 10. What a perfect way to use the Christmas leftovers! Some 30 years later, while I was working in Rome, I was treated to the Italian equivalent, which used courgettes and dolcelatte. Here's my Anglo-Italian version. Leeks, like onions and garlic, help to lower cholesterol and protect against infection, the skin of courgettes is rich in beta-carotene, the Brussels sprouts are a good source of omega 3s and the milk and cheese provide protein and lots of calcium for strong bones.

Serves 4

3 tablespoons olive oil
1 onion, finely chopped
1 leek, finely chopped
2 courgettes, finely sliced
600ml vegetable stock, preferably home-made or use a
    good quality, low-fat cube or bouillon powder
    such as Kallo or Marigold
450ml semi-skimmed milk
12 cooked Brussels sprouts
200g dolcelatte cheese

Heat the oil in a pan and gently sauté the onion and leek until soft but not brown. Add the courgettes, stock and milk. Bring to a boil and simmer very gently for 5 minutes. Add the sprouts and cook for another 5 minutes. Whizz in a blender or food processor until smooth. Return to the saucepan and bring back to a simmer. Crumble in the cheese and stir until dissolved.

very special cullen skink with smoked haddock and salmon

This is my take on the wonderful traditional Scottish soup, Cullen skink. It is healthier made with low-fat crème fraîche than the usual double cream which makes it so unashamedly rich. I've persuaded myself that the benefits of oily fish and the total lack of fat in the haddock balance out the cream. My wife makes it to this day; sometimes we're very good, sometimes we aren't – after all, it is two weeks' worth of the very best omega fats.

Serves 4

50g unsalted butter
1 onion, finely chopped
600ml semi-skimmed milk
3 bay leaves
$\frac{1}{2}$ teaspoon ground nutmeg
275g potatoes, cut into 1cm cubes
350g undyed smoked haddock, skin removed and broken
    along the grain into bite-size pieces
200g low-fat crème fraîche
110g smoked salmon, cut into strips
Dill fronds, to serve

Melt the butter in a large saucepan and gently sauté the onion until soft but not brown. Pour in the milk, add the bay leaves, nutmeg and potatoes and simmer until the potatoes are just starting to become tender – about 10 minutes. Add the smoked haddock and simmer until cooked – about 7 minutes. Lift out the fish. Remove and discard the bay leaves. Mash the potatoes thoroughly. Return the fish and add the crème fraîche or cream. Season to taste and bring quickly to a boil, then take off the heat and add the smoked salmon. Serve hot with the dill fronds floating on top.

rustic cauliflower soup

This fusion soup combines the benefits of cauliflower, often associated with northern climates, and the hot, eastern appeal of chilli and coriander. It is delicious with garlic or cheese croûtons on top. This soup contains lots of minerals, phytochemicals from the onion and garlic, wonderful aromatic oils from the herbs and some extra EFAs from the flax-seed oil and ground flax seeds.

Serves 3–4

2 tablespoons olive oil
2 tablespoons flax-seed oil
1 onion, very finely chopped
1 garlic clove, very finely chopped
½ small red chilli, seeds removed and very
   finely chopped
½ handful each of chopped coriander, parsley and
   mint, leaves only
450g cauliflower florets, very finely chopped
1 litre vegetable stock, preferably home-made
4 tablespoons crème fraîche
2 tablespoons ground flax seeds

Heat the oils in a pan and sauté the onion and garlic gently until soft but not brown. Stir in the chilli, coriander, parsley and mint and continue cooking, stirring, for 2 minutes. Add the cauliflower and stock and simmer until the cauliflower is tender – about 10 minutes. Stir in the crème fraîche and sprinkle over the flax seeds to serve.

asparagus with eggs and purslane

Asparagus has been used as a medicine for around 3,000 years and is known to have been cultivated as a food plant in Egypt since 4,000BC. As well as protein, in surprising quantities for a vegetable, asparagus contains the strongly diuretic asparagine as well as asparagosides – a form of plant hormone – which may explain its long history as an aphrodisiac. Here it is eaten with eggs, vitamin E-rich walnut oil and purslane, an unusual tasting herb which is one of the few plants rich in omega 3 fatty acids.

Serves 4

24 asparagus spears, steamed and left to cool
2 eggs, hard-boiled, cooled and chopped
100g purslane, coarsely chopped
Walnut oil, to drizzle
Freshly ground black pepper

Arrange the asparagus on 4 plates. Sprinkle the tips with the chopped egg. Put a handful of purslane on each plate. Drizzle walnut oil over the asparagus and purslane and finish with a good twist of black pepper.

TIP
Though purslane has been eaten in Britain since the Middle Ages, you won't find it in the supermarket. It's hugely popular in north Africa, and ethnic shops which stock Moroccan or African foods will certainly sell it.

zingy ceviche

Thanks to the growing popularity of Japanese food, the idea of eating raw fish has become increasingly acceptable. This combination of three fish is actually 'cooked' by the marinade, losing none of its nutritional properties and making it easy to digest. As well as protein, B vitamins, iodine and other minerals, this starter will give you a good few days' worth of omega 3 fatty acids.

Serves 4–6

225g fillets each of fresh salmon, red tuna and sea bass
2 teaspoons capers
Few tablespoons semi-skimmed milk
4 lemons
4 limes
6 tablespoons best extra virgin olive oil
3 tablespoons basil leaves, roughly torn
6 sprigs dill, stalks removed
Chunky wholemeal bread, to serve

Get your fishmonger to slice the fish into paper-thin slices – or put the fillets into the freezer for 30 minutes then slice them yourself.

Soak the capers in milk for 10 minutes to remove the salt, then drain and crush lightly in your fingers.

Juice 3 of the lemons and 3 of the limes. Take a wide dish big enough to hold the fish, and mix together the oil, citrus juices, crushed capers, basil leaves and dill. Submerge each fish fillet in the oil and herb mixture and leave in the fridge for at least 6 hours.

Cut the remaining lemon and lime into wedges. Serve the fish garnished with lemon and lime wedges and chunky wholemeal bread.

warm mushroom and red lettuce salad

If you're lucky enough to find real field mushrooms, you'll enjoy their superb flavour, but all mushrooms are nutritious. This dish is rich in protein, phosphorus and potassium from the mushrooms, vitamin C and lycopene from the tomatoes, calcium from the Parmesan cheese and heart-protective chemicals from the garlic. You'll also get a useful amount of EFAs from the flax-seed oil.

Serves 4

2 tablespoons rapeseed oil
1 tablespoon flax-seed oil
2 garlic cloves, finely chopped
12 medium flat mushrooms
1 red lettuce, such a radicchio, divided into leaves
4 tomatoes, sliced
About 100g Parmesan cheese

Heat both oils in a frying pan. Add the garlic and mushrooms and sauté gently.

Divide the lettuce between 4 plates. Arrange the tomato around the outside. Put 3 mushrooms on each pile of lettuce. Drizzle over the garlic oil from the pan. Shave the Parmesan with a potato peeler and scatter on top.

spinach chowder

What could be more soothing than a bowl of hot soup, a traditional comfort and resistance-building food – particularly on a cold evening? But this soup has lots more than the comfort factor going for it. If you can't get green lentils, it would work well with any pulse, but make sure you look at the cooking instructions carefully. Some need soaking overnight and boiling for longer. Surprisingly, spinach is a pretty good source of omega 3 fatty acids – a modest portion provides 0.15g. This may seem tiny compared with a portion of, say, anchovies, but it's still significant. In this recipe it's supplemented by even more fatty acids from the mustard seeds.

Serves 4

2 teaspoons mustard seeds
4 tablespoons olive oil
25g butter
1 medium onion, chopped
3 garlic cloves, finely chopped
175g small green lentils, thoroughly rinsed
$\frac{1}{2}$ teaspoon oregano
650g spinach, thoroughly washed and roughly torn
   (or you can use chard)

Dry-fry the mustard seeds in a frying pan until they pop. Heat the oil and butter in a saucepan, add the onion and garlic and when softened, add the mustard seeds. Add the lentils, oregano and 850ml water. Boil briskly for 10 minutes, then simmer for 25 minutes until the lentils are almost tender.

Add the spinach or chard and continue simmering for another 10 minutes. Liquidise if you like, but this soup tastes great left as it is.

chilled avocado soup

cashew and bean salad

This is one of the prettiest soups you'll find – and as well as being packed with cleansing ingredients, it's also extremely refreshing. It has another advantage if you're entertaining as it can be left in the fridge for a couple of hours before your guests arrive. Don't leave it longer than that, however, or the avocado will start to discolour. It may surprise you that something which is so incredibly healthy can taste so good. There's vitamin E and monounsaturated fats from the avocado, which both protect the heart and reduce cholesterol; cancer-protective lycopene from the tomatoes, immune boosting friendly bugs from the yogurt and lots of EFAs from the pumpkin seeds and walnut oil.

Serves 6

5 large, ripe avocados
1 litre vegetable stock, preferably home-made
Juice of 1 lemon
2 garlic cloves, finely chopped
2 red chillies, de-seeded and chopped
200g tinned organic tomatoes
2 spring onions, roughly chopped
150g natural live yogurt
1 tablespoon walnut oil
2 tablespoons pumpkin seeds

Put the avocado in a blender with the stock, lemon juice, garlic, chillies, tomatoes and spring onions and whizz until smooth. Add the yogurt and whizz again.

Pour into a bowl and leave to chill in the fridge. Dry-fry the pumpkin seeds and leave to cool.

Stir the walnut oil into the soup and serve with the pumpkin seeds scattered on top.

Beans most certainly mean good health. Throughout the Mediterranean, north Africa and the Middle East, variations of bean salads are extremely popular and are one of the staples of 'the Mediterranean diet'. The addition of cashew and pine nuts adds extra protein, fibre, minerals and of course essential fatty acids, to this quick and easy recipe.

Serves 2

2 slices of wholemeal bread, crusts removed
50g unsalted cashew nuts
50g pine nuts
1 garlic clove, finely chopped
3 celery stalks, finely sliced
1 green pepper, seeds removed and diced
3 large spring onions, finely sliced
250g tinned black-eyed beans (drained weight),
    well rinsed
3 tablespoons extra virgin olive oil
1 tablespoon balsamic vinegar

Preheat the oven to 180°C/375°F/gas mark 4.

Cut the bread into 2cm cubes, spread out on a baking tray and put in the oven to crisp – about 5 minutes.

Dry-fry the cashew and pine nuts, tossing occasionally, for about 3 minutes until golden but not burned. Tip into a large salad bowl. Add the garlic, celery, green pepper, spring onions and black-eyed beans and mix thoroughly. Pour in the olive oil and balsamic vinegar and mix well before serving.

indian chard toasts

These very simple Indian delights have the wonderful combination of sweetness from the sultanas, freshness from the chard (or spinach) and spiciness from the garam masala. The pine nuts add protein and essential fatty acids.

Serves 2

25g sultanas
1 tablespoon olive oil
1 garlic clove, finely minced
275g young chard, finely chopped
25g pine nuts
100g tinned chopped tomatoes
$\frac{1}{2}$ tablespoon garam masala
25g parsley, freshly chopped
2 naan breads

Preheat the oven to 180ºC/375ºF/gas mark 4.

Cover the sultanas with freshly boiled water and set aside to stand for 10 minutes. Heat the oil in a pan, add the garlic and sauté gently until softened. Add the chard and cook gently until wilted. Then add the sultanas, pine nuts, tomatoes, and garam masala and heat through. Finally, sprinkle with parsley.

Put the naan bread into a warm oven for about 5 minutes. Top the bread with the chard mixture to serve.

cabbage and beetroot soup

Throughout Europe, cabbage is known as the medicine of the poor – and with good reason. It's rich in vitamin C and antibacterial sulphur, as well as containing large amounts of cancer-protective plant chemicals. Combined here with wonderful beetroot, this delicious peasant soup is good for your blood, prevents constipation and provides some EFAs from the oil, cabbage and seeds.

Serves 4–6

2 tablespoons olive oil
1 medium onion, finely chopped
1 garlic clove, finely chopped
450g raw baby beetroot, diced
1 teaspoon caraway seeds
1.5 litres vegetable stock
2 tablespoons cider vinegar
1 tablespoon flax-seed oil
275g white cabbage, shredded
8 chives

Heat the oil in a saucepan, add the onion and garlic and sweat for 5 minutes. Add the beetroot and caraway seeds and stir over a medium heat for 2 minutes. Add the stock, simmer until tender, then add the cider vinegar. Transfer to a liquidiser and whizz until smooth.

Return the soup to the pan, add the flax-seed oil, and scatter the cabbage on top of the soup. Cover and simmer gently for 5 minutes until the cabbage is cooked but crunchy. Serve with the whole chives arranged on top.

tuna and monkfish tartare

Raw fish isn't to everybody's taste, but this combination of tuna and monkfish marinated in a delicious selection of herbs and extra virgin olive oil then served raw will, I'm convinced, convert the deepest sceptic.

Serves 4

For the monkfish tartare:
Juice of 1 lemon
1 teaspoon ground ginger
1 fat spring onion, very finely chopped
2 tablespoons extra virgin olive oil
350g monkfish tails, very finely chopped

For the tuna tartare:
4 large sun-dried tomatoes, drained and chopped
10 black olives, pitted, thoroughly washed and chopped
1 teaspoon dried or 2 teaspoons fresh chopped marjoram
2 shallots, finely chopped
Juice of 1 lemon
Juice of $\frac{1}{2}$ lime
1 tablespoon extra virgin olive oil
350g red tuna, sliced then chopped

To serve:
4 large dill fronds
1 lemon, quartered
1 lime, quartered

To make the monkfish tartare, mix together the lemon juice, ginger, spring onions and olive oil in a wide dish. Stir in the monkfish and put into the fridge for at least 1 hour.

To make the tuna tartare, mix together the sun-dried tomatoes, olives, marjoram, shallots, lemon juice, lime juice and olive oil. Stir in the tuna and leave in the fridge for at least 1 hour.

Spoon each of the tartares into circular moulds. Top the monkfish with the dill fronds and serve with a slice of lemon or lime on each plate.

TIP
Wrap the tuna in clingfilm and put in the freezer for 1 hour. This makes it easier to slice and chop. Be very careful if you're tempted to use a food processor as it's easy to turn the fish into a purée which loses the wonderful texture.

hazelnut scallops

Queen scallops are a real treat, and as a bonus are packed with omega 3 fatty acids. The nuts in this recipe bring out their delicate flavour and at the same time, boost the essential fatty acid content.

Serves 2

50g unsalted butter
6 queen scallops
Freshly ground black pepper
3 tablespoons fresh thyme leaves
3 shallots, very finely chopped
50g hazelnuts, roughly chopped
1 tablespoon balsamic vinegar
1 bunch rocket

Put the butter into a large frying pan and heat until golden – about 3 minutes – then remove the butter to a bowl and set aside.

Season the scallops with pepper and half the thyme and put into the frying pan. Cook for about 2 minutes on each side, until opaque. Keep in the oven to stay warm. Put the shallots, remaining thyme and hazelnuts into the pan and stir over a medium heat for 30 seconds. Take the pan off the heat, and add the reserved butter and the vinegar.

Divide the rocket between 2 plates and top with the scallops then the shallots, thyme and hazelnuts.

halibut parcels

So simple, yet the wonderful flavour of halibut makes this seem like a very clever bit of cooking. Halibut is an expensive fish, but using small pieces as a starter will feel luxurious without costing the earth. This recipe is a good source of omega 3 fatty acids, with the addition of iron and folic acid from the slightly bitter chicory whose flavour enhances the delicacy of the halibut.

Serves 4

450g halibut fillet, cut into 4 portions
50g unsalted butter, cubed
4 spring onions, cleaned and cut diagonally
1 glass white wine
Juice of 1 lemon
2 heads of chicory, finely shredded
4 teaspoons walnut oil

Preheat the oven to 180ºC/350ºF/gas mark 4.

Wash the halibut and dry on kitchen paper. Cut 4 pieces of kitchen foil large enough to make generous parcels around the fish. Put the a fish fillet on each piece of foil. Divide the butter, spring onions, wine, lemon juice and chicory between the parcels and add 1 teaspoon of oil to each. Close the foil to make loose, airtight parcels and bake in the oven for 20 minutes. Serve the fish in their parcels.

cod roe with onion marmalade and poached eggs

Cod roe is a wonderful source of vitamin D and is rich in essential fatty acids too. It can be difficult to find, but if you're lucky enough to have a good fishmonger near you, he or she will be able to get it for you. This dish is easy to prepare, full of nutrients and has the added piquance of a wonderful onion marmalade.

Serves 4

For the onion marmalade:
50g unsalted butter
1 medium onion, very finely sliced
3 tablespoons redcurrant jelly

700g cod roe
2 organic eggs, whisked
6 tablespoons plain flour
3 tablespoons rapeseed oil
1 large handful each of rocket and watercress,
   thoroughly washed
4 poached eggs (see Tip)

First, make the onion marmalade. Heat the butter in a saucepan and add the onions. Sweat until wilted. Add the redcurrant jelly and stir until well combined. Set aside while you prepare the cod roe.

Slice the cod roe into 1cm slices. Dip them in the egg, then the flour. Heat the oil gently in a frying pan, then add the cod roe slices, cooking for 3 minutes on each side.

Put a pile of mixed rocket and watercress on each plate. Place the cod roe slices on top, then the poached eggs. Serve with triangles of toasted bread and the onion marmalade.

TIP
Most people who cook have their favourite way to prepare poached eggs. This is mine: buy organic, of course, and don't keep the eggs in the fridge. Bring a large pan of water to the boil and add 1 teaspoon of any white vinegar; gently lower in the eggs in their shells with a slotted spoon and nudge them around for about 30 seconds (this helps to keep the whites amalgamated). Remove them, then break them into the water and cook for 4 minutes.

mussel, jerusalem artichoke and leek soup

For most recipes, there's no point in peeling Jerusalem artichokes. It's very wasteful, time consuming and you lose lots of the wonderful nutrients this vegetable provides. All you need is a good stiff vegetable brush and plenty of running water to get them perfectly clean. Remove any of the whiskery side roots, top and tail them and they're ready to use.

As well as the substantial omega 3 from the mussels, this recipe provides great protective phytochemicals from the leek, onion and garlic to fight coughs, colds and viruses.

Serves 6

1 tablespoon butter
2 tablespoons extra virgin olive oil
1 medium onion, chopped
1 leek, washed and chopped
1 garlic clove, finely chopped
700g Jerusalem artichokes, scrubbed, cut in 1cm slices
2 bay leaves
1.5 litres vegetable stock (home-made is best)
Freshly ground black pepper
1kg fresh mussels
Handful of parsley, finely chopped

Heat the butter and oil in a pan and sweat the onions until just soft. Add the leek and garlic, and stir gently for 2 minutes. Add the artichokes, stirring for 2 minutes. Add the bay leaves and stock, season with pepper, bring to the boil and simmer gently until all the vegetables are soft – about 10 minutes. Allow to cool a little before liquidising. The soup should be fairly thick, but if necessary, thin by stirring in a little warm milk.

While the soup is cooking, prepare the mussels. Make sure they're all tightly closed and throw out any which open when tapped on the worktop. Wash thoroughly in a sieve under running water and put into a large flat-bottomed saucepan. Cover with water, turn up the heat and cover. Within 5 minutes the shells will open and the mussels will be cooked. Drain and throw out any that haven't opened.

Pour the soup into bowls, adding the mussels on top and sprinkle with parsley.

light meals

broccoli and cauliflower gratin

A variation on the old favourite, cauliflower cheese. The broccoli and other unusual ingredients give this dish extra bite, extra flavour and extra colour. The American Institute for Cancer Research advises that broccoli specifically helps prevent bowel cancer, but this dish is full of other nutrients too: calcium from the cheese, folic acid from the cauliflower and plenty of EFAs from the walnuts, mustard seeds and, surprisingly, the cauliflower, which in terms of vegetables is a very good source.

Serves 4–6

450g broccoli, cut into florets
450g cauliflower, cut into florets
300ml milk
2 egg yolks
175g low-fat soft cheese
2 teaspoons mustard seeds
50g crushed walnuts
50g Emmental cheese, grated

Preheat the grill to high.

Steam the broccoli and cauliflower for about 7 minutes until just turning soft. Place the milk in a pan, beat in the egg yolks and bring slowly to a boil, stirring continuously. Remove from the heat and add the soft cheese, mustard seeds and half the walnuts.

Arrange the broccoli and cauliflower florets alternately in an ovenproof dish. Pour over the sauce, sprinkle with the rest of the walnuts, then the Emmental cheese. Put under the grill until the cheese bubbles.

sweet potato mash with walnuts and french beans

Sweet potatoes, walnuts and French beans might sound strange, but believe me, this mixture is as delicious as it is healthy. With masses of beta-carotene, energy, protein and essential fatty acids from the walnuts and the oregano, this mash is simple, quick and filling.

Serves 4

3 tablespoons olive oil
1 onion, chopped
1 large garlic clove, chopped
150g chopped walnuts
400g French beans, trimmed and cut into 2.5cm lengths
1 red pepper, diced
Salt and black pepper to taste
1 large sweet potato, peeled, sliced, boiled and mashed
1 tablespoon finely chopped flat-leaf parsley
1 tablespoon finely chopped coriander
2 teaspoons chopped fresh oregano

Heat the oil in a heavy frying pan and sauté the onion, garlic and nuts gently until the onions are soft. Add the beans and red pepper and continue to cook, stirring continuously, until the beans are tender. Season to taste.

Serve on a mound of sweet potato mash, with the herbs scattered on top.

asparagus flan

Asparagus is one vegetable that really is best eaten in season. Nutritionally, the traditional green, English varieties are better than the white spears as they are far richer in beta-carotene. Extremely rich in potassium, folic acid and the natural plant chemical asparagine, asparagus is great for the sex life. The boost to blood flow from cayenne and the vitamin E and EFAs from flax seeds is the icing on the cake.

Serves 6 as a starter, 4 as a main course

Butter, for greasing
1 sheet ready-made puff pastry
20–24 asparagus tips
2 small eggs
200g fromage frais
$\frac{1}{2}$ teaspoon cayenne pepper
1 tablespoon flax seeds

Set the oven to 220ºF/425ºF/gas mark 7.

Grease a 20cm flan tin with the butter. Roll out the puff pastry to 3mm thickness and use to line a tart tin. Arrange the asparagus on the pastry in a cartwheel, green tips facing the rim.

Beat the eggs and fromage frais together. Stir in the cayenne pepper. Pour over the asparagus. Sprinkle with the flax seeds and bake in the oven for 25 minutes until set.

chard with cheese polenta and sesame seeds

Typical peasant food from Italy, this sustaining dish is wonderful as a light lunch or supper – and great to prepare early for when the kids come home from school. Polenta is easily available from all supermarkets these days and is a good source of potassium, iron, B vitamins and fibre. Adding the cheese, for protein and calcium, and the chard for vitamin A, C, zinc and some folic acid makes this an extremely well-balanced meal with the additional benefits of essential fatty acids from the sesame seeds.

Serves 4–6

1 tablespoon olive oil
2 garlic cloves, finely chopped
275g young chard leaves, finely chopped
50g sesame seeds
450g instant polenta
50g mixed Parmesan and Gruyère cheese, grated

Preheat the oven to 200ºC/400ºF/gas mark 6.

Heat the oil in a large frying pan and sauté the garlic gently until soft but not browned. Tip in the chard and sesame seeds, stirring until wilted. Set aside.

Cook the polenta according to packet instructions. Spoon half into an ovenproof dish. Spread the chard mixture over the top and cover with the rest of the polenta and the cheese. Bake for about 15 minutes, until the cheese is bubbling and golden.

chickpea-spinach with mustard seeds

Throughout the Middle East, chickpeas are a staple food, as they are in India, Latin America, Spain and Italy. Inexpensive, nourishing, low in calories, fat-free and fibre-rich, they're a perfect choice for healthy, filling dishes. With a low glycaemic index, they help manage blood glucose levels with their slow-release energy. Like all legumes, they contain plant hormones, which help women more comfortably through the menopause and protect their bones. Surprisingly, mustard seeds are a very good source of essential fatty acids.

Serves 2–3

25g unsalted butter
1kg baby spinach
200g tinned chickpeas (drained weight), rinsed
Large sprig of sage
2 teaspoons mustard seeds, heated in a dry pan until they pop
2 tablespoons extra virgin olive oil
1 tablespoon sesame oil

Melt the butter in a large pan. Wash the spinach (even if you buy packets which say it's ready washed) and add to the pan with just the water clinging to its leaves. Cover and heat gently, shaking the pan occasionally, until the spinach wilts – about 5 minutes. Meanwhile, put the chickpeas into a separate pan with the sage, just cover with water and heat through gently – again about 5–6 minutes.

Drain the spinach, arrange on plates and drizzle with the olive oil. Drain the chickpeas, removing the sage. Pile on top of the spinach, sprinkle with mustard seeds and drizzle with sesame oil.

trout on surprise mushy peas

The surprise is that the mushy peas aren't the normal green variety; in fact, they're chickpeas. I've used them because apart from the protein they contain, they're low in fat and rich in vitamin B, fibre and minerals, especially calcium. They also contain natural plant hormones which help absorption of the calcium so they're really important for women during and after the menopause. Each trout fillet will give you more than a day's worth of omega 3 fatty acids.

Serves 4

4 tablespoons olive oil
1 small onion, finely chopped
1 small garlic clove, finely chopped
1 teaspoon paprika
1 teaspoon chilli powder
225g tinned chopped tomatoes
400g tinned chickpeas
4 pink salmon trout fillets
2 lemons, sliced
4 small coriander stalks

Heat half the oil in a saucepan, and sweat the onion and garlic for about 5 minutes. Stir in the paprika and chilli powder and cook for 2 minutes. Add the tomatoes and chickpeas and simmer until tender – about 10 minutes, adding more water if the mixture starts drying out. Mash the chickpeas roughly.

Pan-fry the trout fillets in the rest of the oil for 2 minutes on each side. Divide the chickpea mash between 4 plates, and top with the fish. Serve garnished with lemon slices and coriander.

scallop stir-fry

All shellfish and seafood are healthy. Don't be put off by the idea that they may contain cholesterol; unless you have extremely high levels or suffer from one of the familial lipid disorders, this is not of any real concern. It's the cholesterol your body makes from saturated animal fats that ends up clogging your arteries. The heart protective omega 3 fats are what you need on a regular basis, and the scallops alone in this dish give you at least half of that. There's also a bit extra in the broccoli.

Serves 4

5 tablespoons rapeseed oil
3 spring onions, sliced diagonally
1 large garlic clove, finely sliced
1 small red chilli, de-seeded and finely chopped
1cm piece fresh ginger root, peeled and grated
3 heads pak choi, quartered lengthways
8 broccoli florets
8 scallops, halved
1 tablespoon freshly squeezed lime juice
2 tablespoons light soy sauce
2 tablespoons finely chopped coriander leaves

Heat 4 tablespoons oil in a wok and sweat the spring onions, garlic, chilli and ginger. Add the pak choi and broccoli and stir until wilted.

Heat the remaining 1 tablespoon oil in another pan, and stir-fry the scallops for a few minutes until translucent. Tip the scallops into the vegetable mixture and warm through for 1 minute, stirring continuously. Stir in the lime juice and soy sauce. Sprinkle over the coriander to serve.

fishy lentils

In my view, pulses of all descriptions should be part of everyone's daily diet. They're packed with protein, are simple to prepare and very sustaining. Here, I've cooked them with tinned salmon for its omega 3 content, carrots and spring onions. Eat some fresh fruit afterwards and you couldn't have a more balanced and protective meal, with protein, vitamins, minerals and the extra vital EFAs from flax seeds and walnuts.

Serves 3–4

125g lentils
3 tablespoons olive oil
3 large spring onions, finely chopped (including green part)
1 egg
150ml milk
2 carrots, grated
175g tinned salmon
25g flax seeds
25g chopped walnuts

Preheat the oven to 200ºC/400ºF/gas mark 6.

Boil the lentils in water, stirring occasionally, until tender – about 20–30 minutes, then drain and put in a shallow casserole dish.

Heat the oil in a saucepan and cook the spring onions until softened. Add to the lentils. Beat the egg into the milk. Add to the lentils, along with the carrots and salmon.

Scatter with the flax seeds and walnuts and bake for 30 minutes in the oven.

prawn and sprout stir-fry

Stir-fries are great for healthy meals in a hurry. You can rustle up something which looks and tastes great in a matter of minutes, contains a minimum of bad fat but plenty of the good essential fatty acids – and leaves you with only one pan to wash up. They're extremely flexible, too – you can use practically any prepared leftover vegetables combined with your favourite sauce to make a standby meal. Prawns and Brussels sprouts may seem strange partners, but believe me, combined with spicy chilli sauce, they're a marriage made in heaven.

Serves 2

275g noodles
2 tablespoons rapeseed oil
4 thick spring onions, quartered lengthways
1 garlic clove, finely chopped
½ sweet, red, pointed pepper, cut into rounds
1 teaspoon dried chilli flakes
200g shelled king prawns, ready cooked or raw
100g button Brussels sprouts, parboiled, drained and refreshed in cold water
2 tablespoons chilli sauce

Cook the noodles according to the packet instructions.

Meanwhile heat the oil in a wok and stir-fry the spring onions and garlic until softened but not brown. Add the pepper and chilli flakes and continue cooking for another minute. Tip in the prawns and stir until heated through – about 2 minutes – if using raw prawns, cook until they turn completely pink. Continue cooking as you add the Brussels sprouts. Take off the heat and stir in the chilli sauce. Return to the heat for 1 minute. Serve the stir-fry over the noodles.

spring onion and anchovy tart

This extremely easy tart, made with ready-made pastry, is perfect for picnics and al fresco summer eating. It can be served warm, but I prefer it cold with a fresh green salad. Anchovies are rich in omega 3 fatty acids, essential for normal cell function and for the healthy development of the brain and central nervous system during pregnancy and breastfeeding. Sadly, they're often underrated because the tinned varieties can be rather salty. The secret is to rinse them well in slowly running water before use.

Serves 4–6

Butter, for greasing
1 sheet ready-made shortcrust pastry
Large bunch spring onions, halved or quartered lengthways (depending on size), retaining about 2.5cm of the green tops
2 x 50g tins or jars of anchovies in olive oil, rinsed well in cold water
300g crème fraîche
2 eggs

Preheat the oven to 220ºC/425ºF/gas mark 7. Lightly butter a large (about 30cm) loose-bottom flan tin.

Roll out the pastry to 3mm thickness and use to line the flan tin. Arrange the spring onions on the top, with an anchovy or two between each slice. Beat the crème fraîche with the eggs until smooth. Pour the mixture over the spring onions and anchovies. Bake in the oven for about 30 minutes until firm. This tart looks and tastes better if you allow the surface to brown slightly but don't burn the pastry.

kipper kedgeree

Salmon, smoked salmon or prawns are very good additions to this dish, especially if you are eating it as lunch or dinner instead of the traditional breakfast. All these fish are extremely rich sources of EFAs.

Serves 2–3

225g undyed kippers
225g long-grain rice
4 hard-boiled eggs, chopped
25g butter, diced
1 teaspoon mild curry powder
1 tablespoon chopped parsley, plus extra for garnish
Freshly ground black pepper
Lemon wedges, to serve

To cook the fish, place in a shallow pan and just cover with water. Bring carefully to the boil then cover with a lid and turn off the heat. Do not disturb it for 10 minutes, by which time the fish should be just cooked through but still succulent.

Rinse the rice carefully and place in a pan with 1.2 litres of boiling salted water. Bring to a simmer and cook gently for 35 minutes. Drain and gently fork up the rice before using.

Skin and flake the cooked fish, checking for bones. Gently stir all the ingredients into the warm rice with a fork. The diced butter should melt into it. Check the seasoning, keep warm and serve with a little extra chopped parsley on top and a lemon wedge.

sardines with yogurt-mustard sauce

herrings in oatmeal

This healthy Mediterranean favourite is little known in this country. That's a shame because sardines are amazingly nutritious, extremely cheap, widely available and very quick to cook. I've paired them here with a sauce that takes less than a minute to make. From a health point of view, you couldn't make a better investment of time or money than make this easy dish. As well as large amounts of omega 3, sardines are a rich source of protein, iron, zinc and vitamin D, which is hugely deficient in most people's diets. This wonderful light meal also contains calcium and gut-friendly bacteria from the yogurt. A glass of wine, a small salad and a hunk of crusty wholemeal bread are all you need to complete a meal that's as good for your soul as it is for your body.

Serves as many as you like

3 sardines per person, cleaned and gutted
Olive oil
2 tablespoons per person plain live low-fat yogurt
½ teaspoon per person Dijon mustard

Preheat the grill to high and line the grill pan with foil.

Place the fish on the grill pan and brush with olive oil. Grill the fish for 2 minutes on each side.

Mix together the yogurt and mustard. Put the fish onto serving plates with the sauce either dolloped over or on the side.

Herrings are the richest source of essential fatty acids, which are so important for brain development and function as well as being naturally anti-inflammatory and helping relieve the problems of dyslexia, ADHD and general learning difficulties in children. They also provide large amounts of the essential vitamin D, without which the body can't absorb calcium to build and maintain strong bones. For the hardy Scots, herrings have long been a staple part of their diet, and they also have the great tradition of using oats, one of the healthiest of all cereals. Serve with warm new potatoes and steamed shredded cabbage sprinkled with caraway seeds.

Serves 4

50g coarse oatmeal
4 twists coarsely ground black pepper
4 large herrings, gutted and split (ask your fishmonger) washed and patted dry
50g unsalted butter
2 lemons, cut in half

Preheat the grill to medium and line the grill pan with foil.

Mix together the oatmeal and pepper. Lay the herrings skin-side down on a grill pan and sprinkle generously with the oatmeal mixture. Dot with butter and grill for about 10 minutes. Put the lemon halves on the side of each plate to serve.

bubble and squeak pancake

It's sometimes hard to get youngsters eating any members of the cabbage family, but cooking them this way makes them palatable to most children. We seem to have lost the art of using leftovers, something our mums and grannies were good at, but this recipe is a great way to finish up yesterday's roast. Here you're providing powerful immune boosting chemicals from the cabbage which not only protect against infections but are known to help prevent many forms of cancer. The potato provides energy and vitamin C and the other vegetables give your children a wide range of vitamins and minerals, especially the beta-carotene which is important for immunity and healthy skin. Surprisingly, even cabbage contains useful amounts of essential fatty acids.

Serves as many as you want

$^1/_2$ cabbage or a good bundle of spring greens or curly
    kale, finely shredded
However much of yesterday's potato is leftover, mashed
    with a little butter and cream
2 tablespoons olive oil
25g unsalted butter
Slices of leftover roast beef, lamb, chicken, turkey or ham
Carrots, celery and red pepper washed and cut into sticks
Plenty of cherry tomatoes

Steam the cabbage until just tender – about 10 minutes. Tip into a large bowl with the potato and mix thoroughly. Use your hands to form into 1cm-thick flat pancakes.

Heat the oil with the butter. Cook the pancakes gently until just brown on the bottom, then turn carefully to brown the other side (5–6 minutes in total). Serve with the meat and vegetables for a delicious lunch or supper.

couscous with shrimps

Shellfish are great if you need a boost but don't really feel like eating a heavy meal. They're light, easy to digest and quick to cook – and you can buy them ready-cooked at any fishmonger's or supermarket. In this recipe I've teamed them with couscous, a wonderful source of slow-release energy. Shrimps are a great source of calcium, iron, iodine and zinc as well as providing plenty of omega 3. Absorption of the minerals is improved by the vitamin C in the other ingredients.

Serves 2–3

300g couscous
8 spring onions, finely chopped
Handful of chives, snipped finely
$^1/_2$ medium cucumber, peeled, de-seeded and cut into
    julienne strips
8 cherry tomatoes, quartered
225g shrimps, cooked and shells removed
8 tablespoons of your favourite vinaigrette dressing
3 tablespoons lemon juice

Wash the couscous thoroughly. Put in a saucepan, cover with water and simmer for 20 minutes, stirring occasionally. Drain and allow to cool slightly.

Transfer to a large bowl and add the spring onions, chives, cucumber, tomatoes and shrimps. Mix thoroughly. Stir in the vinaigrette and lemon juice and serve.

smoked salmon and artichoke benedict

This takes me back to the time I spent in New York, when eggs benedict was practically a legal requirement if you were in the city on a Sunday. Here, I've changed it all around, but it still has many of the basic ingredients. This recipe may sound a bit fiddly, but believe me, it isn't. If a clumsy person like me can open an artichoke, anyone can! This recipe provides a combination of liver stimulants from the artichokes and masses of omega 3 from the salmon.

Serves 4

4 large globe artichokes
3 egg yolks
2 tablespoons lemon juice
75g unsalted butter
4 large slices smoked salmon
4 medium eggs

Put the artichokes in a large pan, cover with water and simmer for about 30 minutes.

While the artichokes are cooking, make the Hollandaise sauce. Put the egg yolks into a large bowl set over a saucepan of simmering water. Add 4 tablespoons water and the lemon juice and bring to a very gentle simmer, whisking constantly. Add the butter, one small piece at a time, still whisking constantly, until thickened. This will take about 15 minutes.

Drain the artichokes upside down. When cool enough to handle, open the outside leaves, pull out the central leaves and furry bits (but do not discard and serve on the side). Tip in the smoked salmon.

Poach the eggs (see page 68 for my method). Add an egg to each artichoke and pour on the Hollandaise sauce.

avocado stuffed with fresh crab

Fresh crab and avocado are two of the most maligned foods. People become obsessive about the cholesterol content of shellfish-like crabs, and women in particular think that avocados are devil's food because they're so fatty and oily and therefore must be left out of any dieter's food list. How wrong can you be. Almost all the fat in avocados is monounsaturated which is the healthy and heart-friendly form. You also get lots of vitamin E and some minerals. An average portion of crab meat provides 0.6g of omega 3 fatty acids which is over half of your daily quota.

Serves 4

2 avocados
1 lemon, squeezed
250g fresh cooked crab meat, shredded
30g low-fat mayonnaise
30g low-fat live yogurt
1 tablespoon capers, thoroughly rinsed and dried
2 spring onions, very finely chopped including green parts
Tabasco sauce, to taste
Freshly ground black pepper
Pinch of paprika

Cut the avocados in half, remove the stones and drizzle with lemon juice (to prevent browning).

Combine the crab meat with the mayonnaise, yogurt, capers, spring onions and Tabasco. Season to taste with black pepper. Fill each avocado with a mound of the mixture. Sprinkle with paprika and serve.

brain balls

Like all oily fish, salmon is a wonderful source of the omega 3, 6 and 9 fatty acids that children's brains need in order to develop and function. With extra energy from the potatoes, protein and protective B vitamins from the eggs, and the immune boosting-benefits of onions, these Brain Balls are a winner with the kids. They're equally delicious cold as well as hot and are perfect for a packed lunch with sticks of cucumber, carrot and a crusty roll. As long as you buy good-quality tomato ketchup without additives and the minimum amounts of sugar and salt, let the kids indulge as it's a super-rich source of lycopene.

Makes 10–12

175g tinned salmon (drained weight)
3 large potatoes, mashed
2 medium eggs
2 spring onions, finely chopped
1 teaspoon finely chopped parsley
About 150ml rapeseed oil
Tomato ketchup, to serve

Mix all the ingredients except the oil and ketchup together. Form into small golf-ball sizes. Heat the oil in a sauté pan and shallow-fry the balls, in batches if necessary. Drain on kitchen paper and serve with the tomato ketchup.

TIP
If you're sending the children off to school with a packed lunch that contains fish, meat or poultry, it's much safer to use a cold bag with a couple of freezer blocks. This is just as important in the winter as most schools are desperately over-heated and the youngsters are just as likely to put their packed lunch on the radiator.

pasta with anchovies and artichokes

I had a dish similar to this when I was working in Rome. My immediate reaction was to say that the only way to eat artichokes was boiled and steeped in butter. How wrong I was! We now grow artichokes in our garden and this recipe is a delight; cut off the young ones early in the season for recipes like this one and save their old relatives until they mature later in the year. That's when you just boil them and dip the succulent leaves in butter – or have them cold with a Hollandaise sauce. Here, this most luxurious of vegetables is teamed with anchovies to bring plenty of omega 3.

Serves 2

4 baby artichokes
½ teaspoon white wine vinegar
175g flat pasta – pappardelle or linguine
50g unsalted butter
3 rashers lean bacon, cut into fine slices
1 garlic clove, finely sliced
10 fresh anchovies – or 50g tinned anchovies, soaked in
    milk for 5 minutes, then thoroughly rinsed
2 tablespoons Parmesan cheese, freshly grated

Cut the spiked tops off the artichokes. Cut into quarters and pick out any furry bits above the hearts. Put into a pan, cover with water, add the vinegar and simmer for 6 minutes.

Remove the artichokes from the pan, reserving the water, and keep warm. Cook the pasta in the artichoke water, according to the packet instructions.

Meanwhile heat the butter in a frying pan and sauté the bacon and garlic.

Drain the pasta and tip into a large bowl. Mix in the bacon and garlic. Top with the artichoke hearts, arrange the anchovies on top and sprinkle with the Parmesan.

shell shocked

If you want to shock your immune system into overdrive, the key mineral you need is zinc – and mussels are an excellent source. So many people only ever eat these delicious molluscs when they go to a restaurant, but this is such a simple dish and incredibly easy to prepare, so do try this at home. The extra benefit of mussels is they're a good source of omega 3 fatty acids and each portion provides half a day's dose. The oregano adds a bit more and you get the extra health benefits from the garlic, onions and parsley.

Serves 4

2kg mussels, washed and scraped – discard any open
   ones which don't close when tapped
25g unsalted butter
1 garlic clove
3 spring onions, finely chopped
½ teaspoon dried oregano
1 glass white wine
4 tablespoons finely chopped curly parsley

Put the mussels into a very large saucepan. Cover with water and cook until all the shells are open and any liquid has drained out. Discard any that are still closed. Strain the liquid through a piece of muslin and reserve.

Put the butter, garlic, spring onions and oregano into a small pan and sweat gently for 2 minutes. Add the reserved liquor, wine and a glass of water. Stir for another minute. Add the mussels, cover and boil briskly for 5 minutes. Empty into a large bowl and sprinkle with parsley.

smokey pasta

It may sound strange to put this amount of smoked fish into a pasta meal, but believe me, it tastes wonderful – particularly with the complementary tartness of the grapefruit and the fresh crunchiness of the French beans. The fish is a wonderful source of omega 3 fatty acids, there's more in the flax-seed oil and believe it or not, you even get some extra in the beans. Each portion will give you two days' worth.

Serves 4

175g spaghetti or spaghettini
1 medium courgette, finely sliced
125g French beans, finely snipped
2 tablespoons extra virgin olive oil
1 tablespoon flax-seed oil
100ml grapefruit juice, preferably freshly squeezed
1 grapefruit, segmented
300g smoked mackerel, flaked
50g smoked salmon, chopped
2 tablespoons finely chopped flat-leaf parsley
2 tablespoons finely snipped chives

Cook the pasta according to the packet instructions. Place the courgette and beans in a separate pan of water and simmer until just tender. Drain the pasta and vegetables and mix together.

Mix the oils with the grapefruit juice. Stir into the pasta and allow to cool. Add the grapefruit, smoked mackerel and smoked salmon. Season and sprinkle with the parsley and chives to serve.

penne with prawns and pesto

Pasta must be one of the easiest meals to prepare – and it's such a comfort food. Here I've combined it with a wonderful mixture of herbs, pine nuts, olive oil and Parmesan cheese – the quintessential pesto mixture – and prawns, which are full of protein and also provide calcium, iron and a good helping of omega 3 fatty acids.

Serves 4

175g penne
2 sprigs flat-leaf parsley
20 sprigs basil
3 tablespoons pine nuts
2 garlic cloves
50g Parmesan cheese, grated
150ml extra virgin olive oil
300g cooked, shelled prawns
Extra chopped parsley, for sprinkling

Cook the pasta according to the packet instructions.

Meanwhile chop the parsley and basil finely or put into the small container of a food processor and whizz for 30 seconds. Add the pine nuts and whizz again. Repeat with the garlic and Parmesan. Add the oil gradually, whizzing all the time. This completes the pesto sauce.

Put the hot penne into a warm serving bowl. Add the prawns, cover and leave for 5 minutes – this is all the 'cooking' the prawns need. Mix in the pesto sauce and serve sprinkled with extra parsley.

skewered sardines

This sardine recipe always reminds me of wonderful holidays in the Mediterranean. I remember one day arriving at Malaga airport; I couldn't wait until I got to my favourite beachside restaurant in Nerja, smelled the sardines cooking on the open fire, took off my socks, put my feet in the sand and... ah yum. Grilled sardines, good bread, a bowl of salad and a glass of wine – so simple and so healthy. You'll find sardines at any fishmongers and most supermarkets, so go on, get out the deck chair and think of holidays.

Serves 4

16 fresh sardines (check to see if the fish you buy has been previously frozen – sardines often are and must not be refrozen)
Olive oil
Coarse sea salt
2 lemons, halved

Preheat the grill to its highest setting.

Soak the 4 wooden skewers in warm water for 30 minutes – this stops them burning. Thread 4 sardines onto each – see the picture opposite. Brush with a little olive oil, sprinkle with salt. Cook the sardines under the grill for 3 minutes on each side. Serve with half a lemon on each plate.

main meals

herby veggie and pasta bake

Italy is one of the better countries for vegetarian travellers. Although there are few native vegetarians, so much of their wonderful Mediterranean culinary repertoire is based on non-meat dishes that there is inevitably a reasonable vegetarian choice in any café or restaurant. Healthy enough on its own, with all the protective benefits of onions, garlic and the vegetables, the white sauce is made here with soya milk for the extra isoflavones. These hormone-like chemicals help protect against osteoporosis and menstrual problems. There are also some essential fatty acids in the oregano, soya milk and flax-seed oil.

Serves 6

For the white sauce:
50g unsalted butter
3 tablespoons flour
$\frac{1}{2}$ teaspoon ground cumin
500ml soya milk

For the lasagne:
1 large onion, finely chopped
1 garlic clove, finely chopped
4 tablespoons flax-seed oil
3 courgettes, diced
1 large aubergine, diced
3 large tomatoes, coarsely chopped
1 tablespoon tomato purée
3 tablespoons fresh oregano, finely chopped
   (or 1 tablespoon dried oregano)
400g dried lasagne, blanched for 3 minutes in boiling
   water – or according to packet instructions
3 tablespoons freshly grated Parmesan cheese
6 fronds fresh dill

Preheat the oven to 220ºC/425ºF/gas mark 7.

To make the white sauce, melt the butter gently in a large frying pan. Take off the heat and stir in the flour and cumin. Return to a gentle heat and cook, stirring continuously, for 2 minutes. Gradually add the soya milk, stirring until thickened.

To make the lasagne, sweat the onion and garlic gently in the oil until soft. Add the courgettes, aubergine, tomatoes, tomato purée and oregano, and continue cooking for 5 minutes, stirring continuously.

Grease a wide, shallow pasta dish with the rest of the oil. Put in one layer of blanched lasagne sheets. Spread on half the vegetable mixture and a third of the white sauce. Add another layer of blanched lasagne sheets. Follow with the rest of the vegetable mixture and another third of the sauce. Add another layer of blanched lasagne sheets and the rest of the sauce, making sure the pasta is well covered with the sauce.

Bake in the oven for 15 minutes. Remove, scatter Parmesan and dill over the lasagne and return to the oven for another 5 minutes until the cheese is golden and bubbling.

tommy tofu

Tofu isn't to everybody's taste, but I'm convinced that's because few people other than those from the Far East know how to cook it. It's practically tasteless, so needs strong flavours to make it more exciting. You can either marinate it yourself – in ginger, garlic and balsamic vinegar – or, as I've done here, buy ready-marinated tofu, and add even more extra flavours at home.

Tofu is a wonderfully healthy food. It's full of phytoestrogens that help regulate hormone levels and is a valuable food for women of all ages as its calcium content helps build strong bones. Tofu is also a good source of omega 3 fatty acids.

Serves 4

3 heaped tablespoons tomato ketchup
2 tablespoons soy sauce
2 tablespoons Worcestershire sauce
1 tablespoon hot chilli sauce
1 teaspoon sesame oil
1 teaspoon chilli oil (see tip)
1 tablespoon rapeseed oil
1 onion, finely chopped
4 tomatoes, coarsely chopped
2.5cm ginger root, peeled and thinly sliced
Handful chopped fresh coriander
225g tofu, cubed

First make the sauce by mixing together the tomato ketchup, soy sauce, Worcester sauce, chilli sauce, sesame oil and chilli oil.

Heat the rapeseed oil in a wok, add the onions and cook till they are soft but not brown. Add the tomatoes, ginger and coriander and stir for 2 minutes.

Pour in the sauce, add the tofu and cook gently for 7 minutes, stirring occasionally.

TIP
Chilli oil is sometimes difficult to find and often expensive, but it's easy to make yourself. When small, hot red chillies are easily available in the shops, buy a few packets – about 20 heads – cover them with freshly boiled water, then drain immediately and thoroughly. Leave to cool, push them into a large bottle, cover with olive oil and leave for at least 2 weeks before use. This oil also gives a really fiery taste to an arrabiata sauce for pasta.

tofu treat

This is a really tasty vegetarian treat, with an Asian flavour. There's plenty of slow-release energy, lots of beta-carotene, vitamin C and other antioxidant nutrients from the vegetables, plus protein, calcium and EFAs from the tofu.

Serves 4

250g tofu
25ml soy sauce
25ml balsamic vinegar
2 tablespoons walnut oil
1 tablespoon crushed capers, soaked in milk for
   5 minutes, drained and rinsed in water
1 tablespoon runny honey
2 tablespoons flax-seed oil
500g prepared stir-fry vegetables
125g rice noodles or rice

Cut the tofu into bite-sized cubes. Mix together the next 6 ingredients and use half to marinate the tofu for at least 30 minutes and preferably 2–3 hours.

Stir fry the vegetables in a little of the remaining sauce for 4 minutes. Add the tofu, in its marinade, and the rest of the sauce.

Reduce the heat and cook for 5 minutes, stirring gently. Set aside but keep warm.

Meanwhile cook the rice noodles or rice according to packet instruction. Divide between 4 plates or large bowls, with the tofu on top.

spiced sweet potato stew

I'm not a vegetarian – give me a bacon buttie any Sunday morning – but I love good vegetarian food and probably don't eat meat at least two or three times a week. This recipe is a particular favourite – something I thought up just because we had some leftovers and store-cupboard staples sitting there waiting to be cooked. With super-healthy ingredients like sweet potatoes and spinach, this is a nutrient-fest, with the added bonus of EFAs from the spices and flax-seed oil.

Serves 4

125g Camargue rice
1 medium onion
1 tablespoon flax-seed oil
3 tablespoons olive oil
1 teaspoon each cumin
$\frac{1}{2}$ teaspoon cinnamon
1 small squash, such as butternut or a chunk of a
   pumpkin, peeled, seeds removed and diced
1 small sweet potato, peeled and diced
230g tinned chopped tomatoes
300ml vegetable stock, preferably home-made
1 teaspoon garam masala
200g bay spinach leaves

Start to cook the rice following the packet instructions – Camargue rice takes about 30 minutes. Sweat the onion in the two oils. Add cumin and cinnamon, stir well and cook for 2 minutes. Soften the squash and sweet potato gently in the onion mixture for 4–5 minutes.

Pour on the tomatoes and stock. Simmer until the potatoes are nearly tender. Stir in the garam masala. Gently lay the spinach leaves on top, cover and simmer for 5 minutes until the leaves wilt into a green covering. Serve the vegetables on the rice.

chickpea and brussels sprout curry

Brussels sprouts team perfectly with chickpeas and this spicy concoction is a real winner. It's warming, satisfying – and tastes just as good cold the following day. As well as phytoestrogens, calcium and protein, chickpeas also contain useful amounts of EFAs, which are enhanced by the unexpected quantities in mustard seeds and cloves.

Serves 4

1 medium onion, coarsely chopped
1cm piece of fresh ginger, peeled and coarsely chopped
1 garlic clove, peeled and coarsely chopped
2 tablespoons olive oil
½ teaspoon ground cloves
10 peppercorns
1 teaspoon mustard seeds
½ teaspoon each turmeric, ground cumin and ground coriander
500g tinned organic chickpeas, drained and well rinsed
100g Brussels sprouts, parboiled for 3 minutes and refreshed with cold water
400g tinned chopped tomatoes
1 tablespoon garam masala
Fresh coriander leaves

Put the onions, ginger and garlic into a food processor and whizz until well combined. Heat the oil in a large frying pan, add the ground cloves, peppercorns and mustard seed and heat gently for 1 minute. Spoon in the onion, ginger and garlic mixture and cook gently for 10 minutes, stirring continuously.

Stir in the turmeric, cumin and coriander and continue cooking, still stirring, for 2 more minutes. Add the chickpeas, Brussels sprouts and tomatoes. Simmer gently for 10 minutes, adding a little water if necessary. Stir in the garam masala. Snip the coriander leaves and scatter over the finished dish.

quick cheat's casserole

If you think a healthy casserole probably takes hours to prepare, just look at this recipe. It cooks in little more time than it takes to lay the table and get out the drinking glasses. Another bonus is that it's full of nutritional benefits and is a key vegetarian dish as it provides plenty of protein. It's also full of fibre, vitamins, minerals, natural plant hormones and EFAs from the soya beans, which you can now buy frozen in most supermarkets. One helping of this nourishing, very low-fat casserole gives you well over a day's worth of EFAs.

Serves 4

1 onion, finely chopped
2 large garlic cloves, finely chopped
4 tablespoons olive oil
400g tinned organic crushed tomatoes
400g frozen soya beans
450g frozen mixed vegetables
1 bouquet garni
2 teaspoons fresh oregano, chopped, or 1 teaspoon dried
850ml vegetable stock, preferably home-made
6 basil leaves, roughly torn
1 tablespoon chopped parsley leaves

Sauté the onion and garlic in the oil until soft but not brown. Pour in the tomatoes with their juices and bring to a simmer. Add the soya beans, mixed vegetables, bouquet garni, oregano and stock to the onions and garlic and simmer for 15 minutes. Sprinkle with the torn basil and chopped parsley to serve.

duck with honey-glazed pumpkin

Without the skin, duck breasts are low in fat and a good source of iron and B vitamins. It may seem strange to serve the pumpkin with honey and sweet spices when cooking a savoury dish, but try it. I first ate this intriguing mixture in a Boer (farmers) café in Stellenbosch, South Africa, which is the heart of the wine-growing region. As in most wine-producing areas, taste and flavour are very important, and these Dutch South Africans know a thing or two about good grub. As well as essential fatty acids in the pumpkin there are also significant quantities in the flax-seed oil.

Serves 2

2 plump duck breasts, cut into thin strips.
2 tablespoons flax-seed oil
1 small pumpkin, peeled, de-seeded and cut into
    small cubes
1 teaspoon ground cinnamon
1 teaspoon ground cloves
1 tablespoon runny honey
Watercress, mint and onion salad, to serve

Pan-fry the duck strips in the oil. Drain on kitchen paper. Set aside, but keep warm.

Put the pumpkin cubes into the pan with the cinnamon and cloves and stir well. Add 2 tablespoons of water, cover and simmer gently until the pumpkin flesh is tender – this should take about 10 minutes, then drizzle on the honey and stir again.

Arrange the duck strips on two warm plates, serve the pumpkin on the side with a watercress, mint and onion salad.

roast duck with berries

Cold duck is delicious for summer parties in the garden and picnics and buffets. Here it's teamed with a wonderfully spicy sauce – with an omega 3 input from the cloves and cinnamon – which complements its rich, sometimes fatty flavour. All you need to add to this dish is a bowl of cold new potatoes and mixed salad.

Serves 4–6

175g mix of cranberries (fresh or frozen and thawed),
    blueberries, raspberries
1 tablespoon honey
2 cloves
Pinch of ground cinnamon
2 white cardamom pods
Pinch of Chinese five-spice
1 glass of port
Knob of butter
Juniper berries
1 crispy roast duck, cold

Put the berries, honey and spices in a pan and add a little water. Over a gentle heat, bring very slowly to the boil, stirring all the time, then add the port. When the berries have reduced to a mush, push through a sieve to remove all the seeds.

Return the sauce to the heat. Stir in the butter to glaze, then add juniper berries and some fresh berries and leave to cool. Pour the sauce over the duck to serve.

TIP
One way to remove duck fat and guarantee lovely crisp skin is to cook it on a trivet in a roasting pan with about 1cm of water in the bottom. Cover the bird with foil so that it effectively steams for the first 30 minutes of cooking, then remove the foil to crisp up the skin. This method works equally well with goose.

stuffed pumpkin or acorn **squash**

Wild rice is a nutritional grain rich in protein and carbohydrate with very little fat. In fact it is slightly better than most other cereals as it is unusual in providing omega 3 and 6 fatty acids which are mostly found in oily fish. It's also high in potassium and phosphorus and an excellent source of the B vitamins: thiamine, riboflavin, and niacin. This is food for the brain as well as the body and makes a tasty, good-looking veggie dish that will satisfy the most devout carnivore. The pumpkin and squash also provide useful amounts of essential fatty acids.

Serves 2

175g mixed wild and white rice
50g raisins
2 tablespoons rapeseed oil
1 medium onion, very finely chopped
1 medium red pepper, finely chopped
1 medium green pepper, finely chopped
50g pine nuts
½ handful fresh parsley, chopped
2 small pumpkins or acorn squashes with the tops sliced
    off and the seeds scooped out with a spoon

Preheat the oven to 200ºC/400ºF/gas mark 6.

Cook the rice until just tender – normally about 20 minutes. Rinse and drain well. At the same time, pour boiling water over the raisins and leave for 20 minutes. Drain.

Put the oil into a large frying pan or wok and gently sauté the onion and peppers. Add the rice and stir well, until covered with oil. Add the raisins and pine nuts and continue stirring for 10 minutes. Add the parsley and stuff the mixture into the pumpkins or squashes. Place into a large baking tin and add about 2.5cm of water. Cover with foil and bake for 40 minutes, until the flesh is tender.

It doesn't matter if you make too much stuffing – it's great cold with a salad the next day or for a packed lunch.

sophisticated salmon

Pretty, pink and affordable as well, salmon is one of the best value sources of protein available in our shops today. It's highly nutritious and quick to make, so it's perfect for a busy weeknight – and there's very little washing up to do afterwards.

Serves 2

2 salmon fillets
About 3 tablespoons olive oil
2 tablespoons breadcrumbs home-made from stale bread ('golden' breadcrumbs from the supermarket won't do)
1 heaped tablespoon fresh parsley
1 heaped tablespoon fresh coriander leaves

Preheat the oven to 190°C/375°F/gas mark 5.

Cut pieces of aluminium foil large enough to make an envelope around each salmon fillet. Brush with some of the olive oil. Place the fillets on the foil.

Grind together the breadcrumbs, the rest of the olive oil, parsley and coriander. Paste on top of the salmon fillets and fold up the foil envelopes.

Cook in the oven for 20 minutes. Open the foil envelopes and sear under a very hot grill for 1 minute. Transfer from the foil envelopes and serve with any sort of green beans or vegetables.

magic mackerel

As a child I used to have very mixed feelings about mackerel. We once went on a holiday to Devon and my father insisted on having mackerel from the local fishermen nearly every day. The trouble was, I was too young – and hungry – to be bothered to take the bones out properly and ended up spitting big mouthfuls back onto the plate. Now that I'm older and wiser – well, sort of – I love it. And of course, today's fishmongers are far more adept at filleting the fish than I was as a boy. This is a terrific helping of heart protection, protein and stimulating nutrients.

Serves 4

4 tablespoons extra virgin olive oil – plus extra for drizzling
2 tablespoons lemon juice
2 tablespoons breadcrumbs
½ teaspoon dried oregano
8 mackerel fillets

Mix the oil and lemon juice together. Stir in the breadcrumbs and oregano and season.

Rub the mixture over the fish and chill in the fridge for 1 hour.

Drizzle the fish with the extra oil and grill under a medium heat for 10–15 minutes each side.

plaice parcels

I absolutely adore fish – and plaice is one of my favourites because of its wonderfully light texture. This recipe contains virtually no saturated fat but even white fish supplies useful, if small, amounts of essential fatty acids. Add the protein, iodine, B vitamins and beta-carotene and you have good health on a plate.

Serves 2

8 large chard (or spinach) leaves, with stalks
4 plaice fillets, scales removed
350ml vegetable or fish stock
1 garlic clove, finely chopped
2 shallots, finely chopped
2 tablespoons olive oil
200g tinned chopped tomatoes
1 tablespoon flat-leaf parsley, chopped

Preheat the oven to 180°C/350°F/gas mark 4.

Blanch the chard for about 3 minutes. Drain, refresh in cold water and pat dry with kitchen paper. (Don't waste the chard stalks, but chop into 2cm lengths, blanch with the leaves, then sauté in a teaspoon of butter. Sprinkle with nutmeg and serve on the side.)

Cut the fillets in half lengthways. Lay each fillet on a chard leaf and roll up reasonably tightly. Put the fillets into an ovenproof dish into which they fit snugly. Pour over the stock. Cover with a lid or kitchen foil and bake for 20 minutes.

Meanwhile sauté the garlic and shallots gently in the olive oil. Stir in the tomatoes and parsley and heat through – about 5 minutes.

Serve the fish parcels with the tomato sauce on the side.

mediterranean barramundi

I first tasted barramundi on a quayside in Sydney when I was visiting my brother-in-law. How fantastic! I even ate it in the same place the following day for breakfast. Happily, thanks to a few enterprising fish farmers here, it's now becoming more easily available in this country mostly because of our dwindling stocks of cod. Barramundi has the same texture as cod, but is slightly sweeter. Here I've adapted one of my favourite South of France cod recipes to take advantage of our fishy friend from Down Under. This is extra healthy as it's one of the few white fish which contains the omega essential fatty acids. There's also masses of vitamins C, A and K from the tomatoes and the sauce. Good on ya, cobber.

Serves 2

450g tinned organic crushed tomatoes
2 garlic cloves, finely chopped
1 tablespoon capers, thoroughly rinsed
2 tablespoons finely chopped parsley
1 teaspoon finely chopped fresh oregano
1 tablespoon extra virgin olive oil
2 barramundi fillets

Preheat the oven to 200°C/400°F/gas mark 6.

Thoroughly mix together the tomatoes, garlic, capers, parsley, oregano and olive oil.

Put the barramundi fillets in an ovenproof dish. Pour over the tomato mixture. Bake in the oven for about 20 minutes, until the fish flakes easily.

louisiana fish with hot southern strawberry sauce

In this recipe I've used simple mackerel fillets, delicate, digestible, very quick to cook and oozing with essential fatty acids. You can use any flat fish and they'll all go wonderfully with this unusual sweet but hot and spicy sauce that combines sumptuous strawberries, hot chillies and horseradish. I'm lucky enough to have this wonderful root growing in our field, but you can buy preserved grated horseradish that works just as well. Do not make the mistake of using horseradish sauce which doesn't have the bite to go with this recipe.

Serves 2

4 mackerel fillets
Freshly ground black pepper and sea salt
3 tablespoons hot chilli sauce
6 tablespoons strawberry jam (buy a really good-quality variety, preferably organic)
1 garlic clove, very finely chopped
3 tablespoons red wine vinegar
2 teaspoons finely grated horseradish
2 teaspoons mango chutney
2 teaspoons lime pickle
2 teaspoons soy sauce
75g wholemeal flour
75g cornmeal
2 organic eggs, beaten
75ml rapeseed oil
250g ripe fresh strawberries, halved

Rinse the fish under cold running water, pat dry and put into a flat dish. Season with fresh ground black pepper, a pinch of coarse sea salt and the hot chilli sauce. Cover and refrigerate for at least 1 hour.

Put the strawberry jam in a small thick-bottomed saucepan with the garlic, red wine vinegar, horseradish, mango chutney, lime pickle and soy sauce. Simmer very gently stirring from time to time.

Mix the flour and cornmeal on a large flat plate. Put the beaten eggs in a shallow rectangular dish. Remove fillets one at a time from the marinade, dip each one into the egg then coat in the cornmeal mixture and shallow fry in a large pan with the rapeseed oil. This shouldn't take more than 2–3 minutes each side. When brown and crisp remove the fish, drain on kitchen paper. Put plenty of the strawberry sauce on each plate, add two fillets to each and garnish with the strawberry halves.

bountiful halibut

Don't worry, you won't be cooking fish with chocolate but you will be using coconut. Of all the white fish, halibut is one of the richest sources of essential fatty acids. It's not cheap but because it is so dense it's filling and there's no waste. Here I've combined the delicate flavours of this fish with the unmistakable taste of coconut and all the digestive benefits of fennel. This is honestly a very easy, very quick but very unusual way of cooking this king of fish. This wonderfully healthy dish is also virtually free from saturated fat, full of protein, calcium and other minerals – and tastes fabulous.

Serves 4

2 tablespoons olive oil
$\frac{1}{2}$ fennel bulb, finely chopped
1 onion, finely chopped
250ml coconut milk
$\frac{1}{2}$ teaspoon nutmeg
1 teaspoon ground cumin
250ml fish stock – of course home-made is always best but you can buy good fish stock or use a cube – not so good
4 halibut steaks
4 tablespoons freshly chopped parsley

In a deep frying pan or sauté pan heat the oil and sweat the fennel and onion till soft. Stir in the coconut milk, nutmeg, cumin and stock. When thoroughly mixed add the halibut steaks, making sure that they are covered with the coconut mixture. Cover tightly and cook gently until the fish is done – not more than 10 minutes. Sprinkle with parsley before serving.

big macks

Mackerel is one of the cheapest and most nutritious of fish and this recipe is a great way to introduce fish to children. Nice texture, no bones, lots of other flavours and of course, a huge amount of the essential fatty acids that youngsters need for their brains to develop and function at their best.

Serves 4

250g cooked mackerel; you could also use mackerel tinned in brine for this dish
175g mashed potato
25g butter, melted
2–3 spring onions, cleaned and chopped
1 tablespoon parsley, chopped
1 tablespoon vegetable stock or milk
1 tablespoon fine oatmeal
Rapeseed oil, to shallow fry
Watercress and tomatoes, to garnish

Skin and bone the mackerel. Flake, and mix with the mashed potatoes and the melted butter. Add the spring onions and parsley. If the mixture is very stiff, moisten with a little stock or milk. Shape into burgers and chill for 30 minutes or more.

When you are ready to eat, dust the burgers with oatmeal and fry till golden brown on both sides. Drain on kitchen paper.

Serve with watercress and slices of tomato. Big Macks can also be eaten cold, in a wholemeal bun or bap, with cress and slices of cucumber.

tropical trout

Trout is plentiful, inexpensive, highly nutritious and in spite of all that, tastes great. Rich in essential fatty acids, an excellent source of protein and B vitamins, and in this recipe, very different from the usual trout and almonds combination. Here we mix the flavours, nutrients and enzymes from papaya with the sharpness of the lime and the fiery taste of Tabasco. This will certainly be good for your soul but it protects the heart and feeds the brain as well. You also get mountains of beta-carotene from the papaya so this not only looks good and tastes good but it does you good too.

Serves 4

4 whole trout, gutted, cleaned and heads removed
Juice of 2 limes
Juice of 1 pink grapefruit
1 tablespoon Tabasco sauce
200ml olive oil
6 tablespoons plain flour, well seasoned with black pepper
   and coarse sea salt
25g unsalted butter
1 glass white wine
2 papaya, peeled, de-seeded and mashed

Put the trout in a large shallow dish and pour over the mixture of juices and Tabasco sauce. Cover and marinate for 1 hour.

Heat the oil in a large frying pan. Remove the fish, roll in the seasoned flour and fry in the oil for 4–5 minutes on each side.

While the fish are cooking, slowly melt the butter in a clean pan, add the wine and papaya and stir over a low heat till warmed through. Serve the fish with the papaya sauce on top.

lamb and lentils

Until recently the only place you'd find a lamb shank was in a genuine Greek taverna where this traditional slow-cooked joint would fall off the bone. Now you can even buy them in the supermarket, though they'd be much better from your local butchers. This is a lean cut of meat which is rich in protein, iron and other minerals and is very slowly cooked here with cabbage that supplies folic acid and some essential fatty acids. Oregano has them too and lentils supply fibre and even more B vitamins to this perfect recipe which gets better the longer it's cooked – ideal when you don't know when everyone's coming home.

Serves 4

2 tablespoons olive oil
4 lamb shanks
2 onions, sliced
500g dark green cabbage, shredded
3 garlic cloves, chopped
1.5 litres lamb, chicken or vegetable stock
2 large carrots, sliced
250g Puy lentils
4 bay leaves
1 generous sprig fresh rosemary
1 tablespoon fresh oregano

In a large flameproof casserole, heat the oil and brown the lamb. Remove and set aside, then add the onion, cabbage and garlic to the pan and sauté until they're all soft. Return the lamb to the pan and add the stock and all the other ingredients. Bring to a simmer, cover tightly and cook gently for at least 1½ hours. To serve, put the lamb shanks on a large platter, use a slotted spoon to put all the vegetables around the lamb, and put the remaining juices into a gravy boat. Make sure you've got plenty of coarse country bread to mop up any liquid.

caribbean fish stew

Traditionally made with snapper which you can sometimes find on UK fish counters, this works just as well with our British cod. The unusual flavours are a delight, plus you will get an enormous boost of essential nutrients. This is a low-fat dish with an excellent balance between the omega 3 and 6 fatty acids that is so important for heart health. You will also get protein, lots of beta-carotene and the other important carotenoids, fibre and circulatory stimulation from the ginger.

Serves 4

3 tablespoons rapeseed oil
1 medium onion, finely sliced
2.5cm fresh ginger, finely grated
$\frac{1}{2}$ pumpkin or 1 acorn squash, peeled, de-seeded
   and cubed
25g pumpkin seeds
1 tablespoon Tabasco sauce
1 tablespoon runny honey
1 tablespoon cider vinegar
500g cod fillet, cut into 6cm wide diagonal strips
Handful coriander leaves, roughly torn

Pour the oil into a wok or large frying pan and sauté the onion and ginger until soft. Add the pumpkin or squash, plus pumpkin seeds, Tabasco, honey and vinegar with just enough water to cover. Mix thoroughly but gently.

Place the fish on top, bring to a boil, then cover and simmer for 20 minutes. When the fish is cooked, carefully remove the fish and set aside. On a warm plate, serve a mound of the pumpkin, with strips of fish on top and scatter with the coriander leaves.

californian chicken

Think of California and instantly images of sunshine, beaches, Hollywood and fat juicy oranges will pop into your mind's eye. In this recipe the combination of chicken, sweet oranges, spices and oregano make a simple and exceptionally healthy casserole. In addition to the protein from the chicken you'll be serving up protection against colon cancer from the turmeric, anti-cold and flu substances in onions and garlic, immune-boosting mushrooms and essential fatty acids in the oregano.

Serves 6

Zest and juice of 2 oranges
3 teaspoons turmeric
4 black peppercorns
2 bay leaves
1 garlic clove, peeled and smashed
6 skinless chicken quarters
3 tablespoons rapeseed oil
1 medium onion, finely chopped
2 garlic cloves, finely chopped
200ml chicken stock, preferably home-made, otherwise
   buy good stock or use an organic low-salt stock cube
150g shiitake mushrooms, sliced
Heaped tablespoon fresh oregano (2 teaspoons if dried)

In a large bowl mix the orange juice and zest, turmeric, peppercorns, bay leaves and smashed garlic, then add the chicken. Make sure the chicken is well coated with marinade, cover and refrigerate for at least 2 hours but preferably overnight, stirring occasionally.

Using a large flame-proof casserole, heat the oil, sauté the onions and chopped garlic till soft then add the chicken pieces, reserving the marinade. Increase the heat and keep turning until the chicken is thoroughly browned. Add the marinade, chicken stock, mushrooms and oregano, cover and simmer for at least 45 minutes. Make sure the chicken is cooked right down to the bone before serving.

barnsley chops with walnuts

It's not always easy to get Barnsley chops, but they do have a lovely flavour. They're a bit fiddly to prepare yourself, so it really is worth finding a good butcher who will do them for you. This dish makes a quick alternative to the traditional Sunday roast – and it tastes great cold, too. The protein teams up with EFAs from the walnuts, antioxidants from the raspberries and the cystitis-fighting chemicals in cranberry juice.

Serves as many people as you like. The sauce ingredients here are enough for two chops, but you'll obviously need to increase the amounts if you're catering for more people.

300ml cranberry juice
1 small punnet raspberries
1 large, juicy peach
About 3 tablespoons olive oil
2 tablespoons walnut oil
3 tablespoons lemon juice
Freshly ground black pepper and sea salt
2 Barnsley chops per person – or one per person
   (large lamb chops will also do)
Large sprig of rosemary
100g walnuts, crushed

Put juice and fruit in a saucepan, bring to a boil and simmer until reduced by half. Blend until smooth. Whisk in 2 tablespoons of olive oil, all the walnut oil, lemon juice, a twist or two of pepper and a pinch of salt. Keep warm.

Preheat a griddle pan or grill. Brush the chops with the rest of the olive oil. Put rosemary on top and cook for 10–15 minutes turning once.

Meanwhile dry fry the walnuts. Put the chops on serving plates with the sauce on the side. Scatter with the walnuts.

chicken with smoked tofu and mango glaze

The combination of meat with sweet fruits is typical of Asia, the West Indies and the Tropics. This recipe, which comes from Cuba, tastes great as well as containing huge amounts of protective antioxidants and nutrients including the essential fatty acids in tofu.

Serves 4

200ml mango juice
4 plump spring onions
1 tablespoon Dijon mustard
Leaves from 1 large sprig fresh rosemary
1 mango, skin and stone removed
4 chicken breasts
150g smoked tofu, cubed

Preheat the oven to 180ºC/350ºF/gas mark 4.

Put the mango juice, spring onions, mustard, rosemary and the flesh of the mango into a blender or food-processor and whizz until smooth.

Put the chicken breasts and tofu into a large, shallow, ovenproof dish and drizzle over the mango mixture. Roast for about 40 minutes, basting frequently, until chicken is thoroughly cooked. Serve with the sauce poured over the chicken and a mixture of brown and wild rice.

desserts

halva hearts with pink sorbet and flax seeds

This divine dessert is the perfect end to any meal. A Middle Eastern favourite for 500 years, it looks romantic, tastes wonderful and, thanks to the honey and sesame seeds, it's an aphrodisiac too. The double dose of sesame seeds and flax seeds makes this unusual sweet a terrific source of omega 3 fatty acids. Isn't it great that anything that tastes this delicious and naughty could be so healthy!

Serves up to 12

For the sorbet:
150ml rosewater
150g golden caster sugar
200ml pink grapefruit juice
Juice of 1 lemon
1 egg white

Boil the rosewater with the sugar until dissolved. When cool, add the grapefruit juice and lemon juice. Whisk the egg white and fold into the mixture. If you have an ice-cream or sorbet maker, follow the manufacturer's instructions. Otherwise, put the mixture into a freezer, and leave until nearly frozen. Take it out, break up the ice crystals and replace it in the freezer. Repeat as necessary until ready to serve.

For the halva:
300g jar tahini
Melted butter (about 25g) to make up 225ml oil and butter mix
175g semolina
250ml runny honey
75g sesame seeds
75g ground flax seeds

Drain the oil from the tahini and put it in a pan with the butter. Heat gently, stirring, until the butter is melted. Add the semolina and cook, stirring constantly until golden – about 20 minutes. Add the tahini and continue stirring until completely amalgamated. In a separate pan, heat the honey and sesame seeds until bubbling – about 10 minutes. Then add to the tahini mixture, stir well and pour into heart-shaped moulds (any shape will do but hearts are more romantic) and leave until set – about 2 hours.

Put 2 scoops of sorbet onto each place with the halva hearts beside. Scatter with the flax seeds and enjoy with a glass of sweet white wine.

TIP
If possible, always try to buy local honey as it helps protect against hay fever.

summer berry dessert

Hungary produces wonderful summer berries and that's where the recipe for this 'fruit soup' comes from. It is overflowing with vitamin C and the protective ORAC antioxidant units (see page 31) There is also a significant amount of omega 3 fatty acids from the strawberries, and research shows that cinnamon can help regulate blood sugar levels and help Type 2 diabetes.

Serves 4–6

500g strawberries
400g mixed summer berries
Juice of $\frac{1}{2}$ lemon
1 tablespoon runny honey
1 teaspoon ground cinnamon
1 heaped teaspoon arrowroot
4 tablespoons natural live yogurt

Put the fruit, lemon juice, honey and cinnamon into a large pan with 700ml water. Simmer until the fruit is soft. Push through a sieve with a wooden spoon and return to the pan.

Mix the arrowroot with a little water to make a firm paste. Add to the pan and bring slowly to a boil, stirring continuously. Serve cold, with a spoonful of yogurt in each bowl.

matzo fritters with strawberry purée

Matzo is the unleavened bread that was eaten by Jews as they fled from Egypt – there was not time to let the dough rise, so it ended up as a flat, crisp bread. They can be found in most supermarkets together with the crushed version, matzo meal. There are many recipes for cooking with matzo. Here's my favourite, with the luscious flavour, and essential fatty acids of strawberries.

Serves 4–6

100g caster sugar
4 tablespoons runny honey
Juice and zest of 1 lemon
150g ripe strawberries, hulled and puréed
4 eggs
6 tablespoons medium matzo meal
About 400ml rapeseed oil

Put the sugar, honey and lemon juice into a pan with 200ml water. Bring to a boil, stirring, until the sugar and honey are dissolved. Add the strawberry purée, set aside and keep warm.

To make the fritter mixture, separate the eggs and whisk the whites until stiff. In another bowl, beat the yolks gently with the lemon zest, and fold them into the whites. Sift the matzo meal on top and mix thoroughly.

Heat the oil in a large, wide frying pan. Drop in the fritter mixture, a tablespoon at a time and shallow-fry, turning once, until golden – you'll need to do this in batches. As you're cooking, drain each batch of fritters on kitchen paper and keep warm. Arrange the warm fritters on a serving dish and pour over the strawberry purée.

oat 'n' fruit crumble

What a treat this popular favourite is – especially in autumn, when you can pick the blackberries yourself. If you can't get hold of wild blackberries, shop-bought fruit, even if it's from the freezer cabinet, will do. This is a healthy variation as it uses porridge oats mixed with nuts and seeds for the topping and is extremely low in saturated fat. Add a dollop of organic fat-free bio yogurt if you want to be extra healthy, but of course the traditional custard or cream make a dessert all the family will love. At least you'll know they will be getting their EFAs from the nuts and seeds.

Serves 4

Soft unsalted butter, for greasing
2 cooking apples, cored, peeled, halved and sliced
1 heaped tablespoon dark Barbados sugar
About 450g blackberries – defrosted if you're using
    frozen fruit
100g porridge oats
100g ground almonds
2 tablespoons ground flax seeds
2 tablespoons flaked almonds
About 2 tablespoons runny honey – using a squeezy
    plastic container is easier
30g unsalted butter, chilled and cut into tiny pieces

Preheat the oven to 200ºC/400ºF/gas mark 6. Lightly grease a deep ovenproof dish with butter. Cover the bottom with sliced apple. Sprinkle with the sugar. Cover with the blackberries, leaving at least 2.5cm at the top of the dish. Mix together the porridge oats and ground almonds and spread on top of the fruit. Sprinkle over the ground flax seeds, scatter over the flaked almonds, drizzle with the honey and dot with the chilled butter. Bake for 20–30 minutes until the nuts are golden.

spicy nut pyramids

Most people find it hard to imagine that any type of biscuit could be healthy but here's one you can eat with a clear conscience. Yes, they do contain sugar but they're gluten-free, wheat-free and dairy-free. They provide both essential and monounsaturated fatty acids so they're good for the whole central nervous system and the heart. You'll also get some B vitamins, some vitamin E and lots of protein.

Makes 10–12

Soft unsalted butter, for greasing
2 large eggs, beaten
225g ground hazelnuts
50g ground walnuts
175g brown caster sugar
1 teaspoon ground ginger
1 teaspoon ground cloves
Icing sugar, for dusting

Preheat the oven to 180ºC/350ºF/gas mark 4. Grease a baking sheet.

Break the eggs into a bowl and beat in the nuts, sugar and spices until you have a fairly thick dough. Put tablespoonfuls of the mixture on the baking sheet, making sure they're well spaced out, and shape each one into a pyramid. Place in the oven for 25–30 minutes until golden. When cooked, leave to cool on a wire rack and lightly dust with icing sugar.

nutty fruit terrine

This delicious dessert is bound to impress, yet really simple to make. The combination of fruits will give you almost a day's worth of protective ORACs (see page 31) thanks to their high vitamin C content and other protective constituents. The pistachios and pecans add an unusual flavour and also a small amount of EFAs.

Serves 4–6

1 kiwi fruit, peeled, quartered lengthways and sliced (not too thinly)
About 3 heaped tablespoons fresh blueberries
About 3 heaped tablespoons frozen cranberries, defrosted
About 2 heaped tablespoons pistachio nuts, shelled
2 tablespoons lime or lemon juice
300ml white wine
2 tablespoons runny honey
Gelatine powder – enough to set just over 300ml
About 3 heaped tablespoons pecan nuts, chopped

Line a large loaf tin with clingfilm. Arrange the fruit and pistachios inside.

Mix the juice and wine in a saucepan over a low heat. Add the honey, stirring until dissolved. In a separate bowl, sprinkle the gelatine over 4 tablespoons water (or as per packet instructions) until swollen.

Pour the gelatine mixture into a small saucepan and warm gently, stirring all the time, until completely dissolved. Stir into the wine mixture and pour over the fruit. Cover with clingfilm and leave in the fridge until set (about 2 hours).

Remove the top layer of clingfilm, invert the terrine onto a serving dish and remove the rest of the clingfilm. Scatter with the pecan nuts.

italian rhubarb pudding

I'm not normally a pudding person – cheese is more my bag – but this pud, which my wife makes all through the summer, even when the rhubarb from our garden is getting a bit stringy, is to die for. I have to admit, however, that it's far more delicious early in the year when the rhubarb we've forced through the winter is still young, tender and looking like pink champagne.

Serves 6

1 standard panettone
About 75g unsalted butter
700g young rhubarb, cut into 1cm chunks
2 tablespoons flax seeds
425ml double cream
250ml milk
4 large eggs
3 tablespoons amaretto or dry sherry

Preheat the oven to 190ºC/375ºF/gas mark 5.

Cut a 1cm slice off the bottom of the panettone, then another, and a further 1cm slice off the top (keep the rest for dunking in your coffee or toasting for breakfast). Butter the bottom slice on the cut edge, and put butter-side down in an ovenproof dish just big enough to hold it. Scatter over half the rhubarb and sprinkle with half the flax seeds. Butter the second slice of panettone on both sides and place on top. Cover with the rest of the rhubarb and sprinkle with remaining flax seeds. Butter the top slice of panettone on the cut edge, and place on top, butter-side down.

Whisk together the cream, milk, eggs and amaretto or sherry. Pour over the pudding and refrigerate for 1 hour. Fill a roasting pan with 2.5cm water. Set the pudding in the water. Cover with foil and put into the oven. After 30 minutes, remove the foil, then cook for another 30 minutes until golden on top.

sweet and sour strawberries

The popular drink granita, a bit like a half-frozen lemon sorbet, is served at practically every café around the Mediterranean. Add fresh strawberries and their delicious sweetness will contrast with the sharpness of the lemon juice. This dish has masses of vitamin C and also anti-inflammatory agents, making it a great treat, especially for those who suffer from arthritis. It's also pretty good for almost everyone else, thanks to the small but useful amount of EFAs in strawberries.

Serves 2

50g caster sugar
Juice of 4 unwaxed lemons
350ml mineral water
12 strawberries
4 langues du chat biscuits

Place the sugar and lemon juice in a pan and heat until the sugar has dissolved. Leave to cool, then add the mineral water. Put the mixture into a freezer-proof container and freeze for 2 hours, breaking up the crystals with a fork every 30 minutes.

Put 4 strawberries in the bottom of 2 tall sundae glasses. Fill with the granita mixture. Top with rest of the fruit and serve with biscuits on the side.

simple raspberry tarts

These drop-dead gorgeous show-off tarts are simplicity itself. You'd pay a fortune for them at a posh deli, but you can make them at home in half an hour. And isn't it great that something this tasty also includes EFAs from the tahini?

Serves 4

Butter, for greasing
1 sheet ready-made shortcrust pastry, defrosted
    if frozen
2 tablespoons tahini
1 large punnet raspberries
2 free-range organic eggs
200g crème fraîche
2 tablespoons caster sugar
1 teaspoon vanilla extract

Preheat the oven to 200ºC/400ºF/gas mark 6. Butter 4 loose-bottomed 10cm flan tins.

Roll out the pastry to a 3mm thickness and use to line the tart tins. Spread the tahini over the pastry. Arrange the raspberries on top. Beat together the eggs, crème fraîche, sugar and vanilla extract and pour over the raspberries. Bake for 20 minutes in the oven until set.

berry quiche

This super treat, which is delicious and good for you at the same time, is so simple. Yet it looks as if a serious pastry cook has been at work in your kitchen. You can start from scratch and make the pastry yourself – or use ready-made pastry which obviously saves a great deal of time and effort. You can make one large quiche if you like, but I always think individual ones look so much nicer. They contain lots of calcium, good bacteria from the yogurt and some omega 3s from the strawberries and seeds.

Serves 2

Butter, for greasing
1 sheet frozen shortcrust pastry, defrosted
Milk, for brushing
100g feta cheese
100g fat-free Greek yogurt
2 medium eggs
1 tablespoon double cream
2 tablespoons poppy seeds
1 small punnet strawberries, cut in half
2 sprigs fresh mint

Preheat the oven to 180ºC/350ºF/gas mark 4. Use the butter to grease two 10cm fluted quiche tins with removable bottoms.

Roll out the pastry to a 3mm thickness and cut into rounds about 2.5cm larger than the tins. Press it into the tins, working it round the circumference with your fingers. Brush with a little milk, cover with foil and bake for about 20 minutes until the pastry just starts to bubble.

Put the cheese, yogurt, eggs and cream into a blender and whizz until thick and creamy. Fill both pastry cases with the mixture, sprinkle with the poppy seeds and return to the oven for 20 minutes until the filling is golden. Arrange the strawberries cut-side down in circles on each tart and finish under a hot grill until the fruit just starts to bleed. To serve, decorate with the mint sprigs.

essential cranberry muffins

Perfect comfort food, these muffins knock spots off any shop variety – and they don't involve hours sitting around waiting for them to bake. Here I've added a healthy touch by using a mixture of oils with all their essential fatty acids instead of using the normal butter. Yes, there is quite a lot of sugar, but we all deserve a treat from time to time! The cranberries also contain those all-important antioxidants and antibacterial substances.

Makes 8

275g plain flour
2 teaspoons baking powder
150g golden caster sugar
1 teaspoon ground flax seeds
1 teaspoon allspice
1 egg
20ml flax-seed oil
300ml olive oil
Zest of 2 lemons
150g cranberries (frozen are fine as long as they're fully
    defrosted and very thoroughly dried on kitchen paper)
Unsalted butter, for greasing
Cream or custard, to serve

Preheat the oven to 200ºC/400ºF/gas mark 6.

Sift the flour, baking powder, sugar, flax seeds and allspice into a bowl. In another bowl, whisk the egg with the oils and lemon zest. Combine the contents of both bowls. Stir in the cranberries carefully, trying not to break up the fruit. Spoon into 8 muffin cases or lightly greased muffin tins, filling them only two-thirds full. Bake for about 15 minutes until just firm. Turn out onto a wire rack to cool. Serve with cream or custard.

super-seedy loaf

As well as plenty of EFAs, this cake provides relief from menopausal symptoms and PMS. Barlean's Forti-Flax is a natural source of essential fatty acids and phytoestrogens which can also be sprinkled on your breakfast cereal. It's available from www.healthyandessential.com

Makes 1 loaf

100g soya flour
100g wholewheat flour
100g porridge oats
100g Barlean's Forti-Flax (see above)
50g linseeds
25g sunflower seeds
25g pumpkin seeds
10g sesame seeds
$\frac{1}{2}$ teaspoon nutmeg
$\frac{1}{2}$ teaspoon cinnamon
$\frac{1}{2}$ teaspoon ground ginger
2 pieces stem ginger, chopped
200g raisins
2 free-range organic eggs
150ml semi-skimmed milk
150ml soya milk
1 tablespoon malt extract
50g flaked almonds

Preheat the oven to 190ºC/375ºF/gas mark 5. Line a loaf tin or round tin with greaseproof paper.

Put all the dry ingredients except the almonds into a large bowl and mix thoroughly. Stir in the ginger and raisins. Add the eggs, milk and malt extract. Mix well and leave to soak for 30 minutes. If the mixture is too stiff, add more soya milk. Spoon into a loaf tin and press the almonds into the top. Bake in the oven for about $1\frac{1}{4}$ hours. Turn out and leave to cool.

peanut brittle bananas

This gorgeous pudding is far healthier than you might think. The fats and oils in the seeds and peanuts are rich in minerals, monounsaturated fats and vitamin E which all help to protect the heart. The banana provides potassium, B vitamins and easily converted energy. Although it is made with butter and sugar, as an occasional treat this is better than most, so don't feel guilty!

Serves 2

75g caster sugar
25g unsalted butter
50g crunchy organic peanut butter
2 whole bananas, peeled
25g sesame seeds, dry-fried

Put the sugar, butter and 1 tablespoon water into a deep non-stick frying pan and heat very gently, stirring all the time. As the sugar and butter dissolve, a toffee starts to form. Now add the peanut butter and stir thoroughly. Add the whole bananas, turning every minute or so to coat evenly.

Carefully remove the bananas from the pan with a slotted fish slice and place on cold plates. Pour over the sauce left in the pan, sprinkle with the sesame seeds and within a few seconds the mixture will set around the bananas, forming a wonderful toffee peanut brittle.

apple syllabub with pine nut topping

Syllabubs look fancy, and are great if you're having friends to lunch or dinner, because you can make them well in advance. I make the components for this healthier syllabub (healthier because it's made with yogurt rather than cream) the night before, assemble it in the morning and put it in the fridge to chill. It incorporates cholesterol-lowering pectin from the apples, calcium and friendly bugs from the yogurt, and protein and EFAs from the pine nuts.

Serves 3

2 Bramley apples, cored, peeled and finely diced
2 tablespoons Greek honey
3 tablespoons golden caster sugar
75ml dry cider
250g low-fat Greek yogurt
4 gingernut biscuits
3 heaped tablespoons toasted pine nuts

Put the apples, honey, sugar and cider into a pan and simmer gently until they make a smooth purée. Leave to cool completely. Mix together half the cooled apple purée with the yogurt, reserving the rest of the apple purée. Crush the biscuits in a blender.

To assemble, put about 2 tablespoons of the reserved apple purée into 3 sundae glasses – or use large wine glasses. Add the crushed biscuits. Top with most of the yogurt and apple mixture then the rest of the reserved apple purée. Add another thin layer of the yogurt and apple mixture. Finish with the pine nuts and chill for at least 1 hour.

TIP
If ginger biscuits aren't to your liking, try using digestives, chocolate chip cookies or even peanut biscuits.

afro-asian rice pudding

Fusion cooking is such a wonderful reflection of the multi-cultural society we're so lucky to live in. This recipe comes from one of my patients, who was born in India and brought up in Morocco, hence the rice and carrots combined with orange blossom water and cloves. These nutritious ingredients are supplemented with pistachios, which provide protein along with significant quantities of vitamin E and potassium, both of which protect the heart and help lower cholesterol. Together with the cloves, they also provide useful amounts of EFAs.

Serves 4–6

850ml semi-skimmed milk
2 tablespoons basmati rice
450g carrots, grated
$\frac{1}{2}$ teaspoon ground cardamom
1 teaspoon ground cloves
75ml orange blossom water
3 tablespoons double cream
4 tablespoons pistachio nuts, chopped

Boil the milk in a large saucepan. Add the rice and stir for 2 minutes. Turn down to a simmer and cook for a further 20 minutes, stirring frequently.

Add the carrots and cook for another 15 minutes until you have a sauce-like consistency – the carrots will absorb the milk.

Stir in the cardamom, ground cloves, orange blossom water and cream. Put into individual ramekins and chill thoroughly. Serve sprinkled liberally with pistachios and be prepared for a surprising taste sensation.

nutty winter compote

This is a perfect dessert as it can be eaten at any time of the day and is just as tasty hot or cold. It's also good for breakfast with yogurt. Each portion provides an entire day's dose of ORAC units (see page 31), which protect against ageing, cell damage, cancers and even wrinkles. Vitamins, minerals and instant energy from the fruit sugars are all there, with some protein, essential fatty acids and vitamin E from the almonds and walnuts. You'll get a bonus from the cinnamon too, as it's not only antibacterial, but also an effective mood enhancer.

Serves 6–8

225g stoneless prunes
225g dried apricots
225g dried pears
225g dried apples
50g raisins
50g sultanas
50g chopped walnuts
50g flaked almonds
2 lemons, sliced
3 large pinches ground cinnamon
3 large pinches ground nutmeg
1 tablespoon brandy (optional)
500ml freshly-squeezed orange juice

Preheat the oven to 180ºC/350ºF/gas mark 4.

Mix all the dried fruit and nuts in a large bowl. Put half in the bottom of a large casserole. Cover with half the lemon slices. Add the rest of the fruits and nuts and cover with the remaining lemon slices. Sprinkle with the spices, add the orange juice and brandy if using and bake for 20 minutes in the oven.

smoothies and juices

veggie reviver

As well as the omega 3 boost from the delicious pistachio nuts, this unusual tomato juice has masses of potassium, lots of vitamins C and E, folic acid, magnesium and a huge boost of lycopene to protect against some types of cancer. It's refreshing and cleansing and helps women who are prone to fluid retention at the time of their periods.

Makes 1 large glass

1 carrot
4 large ripe plum tomatoes
2 sticks celery, with leaves
Handful of flat-leaf parsley
Juice of 1 lemon
Juice of $\frac{1}{2}$ lime
1 tablespoon pistachio nuts, crushed
Freshly ground black pepper

Wash the vegetables. Peel the carrot if it's not organic. Put all the ingredients straight into a juicer. Mix well and add the lemon juice. Serve with a twist of black pepper.

pollytox

In the middle of London's leafy Hampstead sits one of my favourite cafés, Polly's Tea Rooms. The good old-fashioned food and drink they serve always goes down a treat. This detox drink has been on their menu for as long as I can remember. With all the energy from the natural sugars in the grapes, the protective chemicals in the grape skin, the cleansing fibre in the apples and a huge dose of vitamin C from the lemons, this 'Pollytox' is all you need for a refreshing energy boost. No fatty acids in this one, but lots of other goodies.

Makes 2

500g white grapes
2 green apples
Juice of 2 lemons

Juice the grapes and apples. Stir and add the lemon juice. Stir and serve over ice.

tomatoes plus

Throughout the southern Mediterranean, tomatoes, oregano and basil are practically inseparable. This mind and body juice is super-rich in minerals to invigorate tired muscles, and full of calming essential oils from the basil to revive the flagging mind and spirit. As well as flavour, the oregano contributes some omega 3s. The other great bonus is lycopene, an important carotenoid that gives ripe tomatoes their deep red colour. This nutrient protects against prostate cancer in men and breast cancer in women.

Makes 1

4 large ripe plum tomatoes
1 carrot
1 stick celery
Handful of fresh basil
Juice of $\frac{1}{2}$ lemon
Dash of Worcester sauce
Freshly ground black pepper
1 teaspoon chopped fresh oregano per glass

Juice the tomatoes, carrot, celery and basil, putting a few basil leaves between each piece of carrot or celery to make sure they're processed. Stir in the lemon juice, Worcester sauce and a twist of black pepper and sprinkle each glass with oregano.

summer burst

'Oil in a cooling juice?' I hear you cry... but flax-seed oil has practically no taste and combines well with this cornucopia of fresh fruit, salad and herbs.

Makes 2 large glasses

4 apples, quartered (no need to peel or core)
1 small pineapple, peeled
15cm piece of cucumber
Small handful of coriander leaves
1 tablespoon flax-seed oil
300ml yogurt or mascarpone cheese
3 strawberries, cut in half

Put the apples, pineapple, cucumber and coriander leaves through a juicer. Stir in the flax-seed oil and yogurt or mascarpone. Serve with the strawberries floating on top.

green dream

This combination is a pretty good substitute for lunch if you're trying to lose weight healthily. It's bursting with all sorts of nutrients and, thanks to the broccoli, is a good source of omega 3s. In addition, watercress contains a specific chemical which is believed to protect against lung cancer. If you're daft enough to smoke, this should be a vital part of your regular diet.

Makes 2 glasses

175g broccoli spears
1 apple, preferably Cox's
1 Comice pear
150g watercress

Put all the ingredients through a juicer. Chill and stir well before serving.

spice island special

You can almost hear the sound of breakers on a coral reef when you smell this mixture of coconut, cinnamon and cloves. The addition of rum is entirely optional but totally delicious.

This drink is of particular value to women – the amazing benefits of soya protect against breast cancer, osteoporosis and menopause problems. It also contains protein, calcium, iron, some B vitamins and plenty of essential fatty acids. The yogurt provides calcium, and the cinnamon, cloves and probiotic bacteria are all digestive aids.

Makes 1

10ml soya milk
5ml coconut milk
5g frozen low-fat live yogurt
$\frac{1}{2}$ teaspoon ground cinnamon, plus extra to decorate
$\frac{1}{4}$ teaspoon ground cloves
Shot of Jamaican rum (optional)

Blend all the ingredients with a handful of ice cubes. Pour into glasses and decorate with a pinch of cinnamon.

paradiso

Even the preparation of the tropical fruits for this juice makes you feel great! Whipped into a cooling frothy shake with live yogurt, this combination is invigorating, restoring and protective. It's wonderful for children, though some prefer it without the ginger, and perfect for women in the early stages of pregnancy as the ginger helps prevent early morning sickness.

You'll be getting vitamins A, B and C, calcium, and other minerals, but most importantly the healing enzyme bromelain from the pineapple. All these nutrients combine to make this a real blockbuster. Combined with the beneficial bacteria in yogurt and the useful essential fatty acids in the tofu, it's one of the healthiest smoothies you can drink.

Makes 2 large glasses or 4 wine glasses

1 mango, peeled and stoned
1 pineapple, peeled
2.5cm piece of fresh ginger root
1 lime, peeled
150g fat-free Greek yogurt
50g plain tofu
2 ice cubes per glass

Juice the mango, pineapple, ginger and lime. Blend with yogurt and tofu and pour over ice cubes.

popeye

Almost everyone loves apple juice. But adding spinach? In fact, spinach is delicious juiced, so don't knock it till you've tried it. This is a great slimming drink as it provides lots of essential nutrients – including a modest amount of omega 3s in the spinach – but very few calories. Nutmeg, by the way, contains the 'happy' chemical myristicin, which is mood enhancing.

Makes 2 glasses

175g baby spinach leaves
1 small red pepper, de-seeded
3 apples, preferably Cox's, quartered
Pinch of nutmeg
Pinch of sesame seeds

Put the first three ingredients through a juicer. Serve with the nutmeg and sesame seeds sprinkled on top.

hot soya soother

This comforting milk drink reminds me of my childhood, when I was often given a cup of hot milk before bedtime to help me sleep. This hot drink, however, is very 'grown up', with the sophisticated but delicate flavour of saffron combining wonderfully with the soya milk and honey. You even get a little omega 3 from the nuts.

Makes 2 glasses

Tiny pinch saffron
500ml soya milk
2 tablespoons honey
50g pistachios

Put the saffron into a pan with a little of the soya milk. Stir until the saffron is almost dissolved.

In a separate pan, bring the rest of the milk to a boil and turn down to simmer. Add the honey and stir until dissolved. Pour in the saffron milk and heat through gently if necessary. Serve with the pistachios scattered on top.

clove and apple tea

Fruit and herbal teas are very popular these days, but not many people realise how easy they are to make at home. This combines those lovely English Cox's apples with the spiciness of cloves, which as well as being a reasonable source of omega 3s, are a useful aid to digestion.

Makes 2 glasses

4 whole cloves
4 apples, preferably Cox's, chopped
2 teaspoons ground cloves

Put the whole cloves and apples into a saucepan. Pour on about 450ml of cold water, bring to a boil and simmer, covered, for 30 minutes. Sieve and serve hot, with the ground cloves sprinkled on top.

banana booster

This might sound like a kid's party treat – and most children will love it – but it's also a real energy boosting and nutritious drink. It's good at any time of day, but thanks to the slow-release calories and cramp-preventing potassium from the bananas, this is a particularly good smoothie to have before you exercise. The peanut butter (use organic low-salt if possible) contains heart-protective phytochemicals and the strawberries offer a modest amount of essential fatty acids.

Makes 2

5 apples, quartered
8 strawberries
2 bananas, peeled
1 tablespoon smooth peanut butter

Juice the apples and strawberries, then blend with bananas and peanut butter.

index

conversion tables

Weight (solids)

7g	1/4oz	375g	13oz
10g	1/2oz	400g	14oz
20g	3/4oz	425g	15oz
25g	1oz	450g	1lb
40g	1 1/2oz	500g (1/2kg)	18oz
50g	2oz	600g	1 1/4lb
60g	2 1/2oz	700g	1 1/2lb
75g	3oz	750g	1lb 10oz
100g	3 1/2oz	900g	2lb
110g	4oz (1/4lb)	1kg	2 1/4lb
125g	4 1/2oz	1.1kg	2 1/2lb
150g	5 1/2oz	1.2kg	2lb 12oz
175g	6oz	1.3kg	3lb
200g	7oz	1.5kg	3lb 5oz
225g	8oz (1/2lb)	1.6kg	3 1/2lb
250g	9oz	1.8kg	4lb
275g	10oz	2kg	4lb 8oz
300g	10 1/2oz	2.25kg	5lb
310g	11oz	2.5kg	5lb 8oz
325g	11 1/2oz	3kg	6lb 8oz
350g	12oz (3/4lb)		

Volume (liquids)

5ml	1 teaspoon	325ml	11fl oz
10ml	1 dessertspoon	350ml	12fl oz
15ml	1 tablespoon	370ml	13fl oz
	or 1/2fl oz	400ml	14fl oz
30ml	1fl oz	425ml	15fl oz or
40ml	1 1/2fl oz		(3/4 pint)
50ml	2fl oz	450ml	16fl oz
60ml	2 1/2fl oz	500ml (0.5l)	18fl oz
75ml	3fl oz	550ml	19fl oz
100ml	3 1/2fl oz	600ml	20fl oz
125ml	4fl oz		(1 pint)
150ml	5fl oz (1/4 pint)	700ml	1 1/4 pints
160ml	5 1/2fl oz	850ml	1 1/2 pints
175ml	6fl oz	1 litre	1 3/4 pints
200ml	7fl oz	1.2 litres	2 pints
225ml	8fl oz	1.5 litres	2 1/2 pints
250ml (0.25l)	9fl oz	1.8 litres	3 pints
300ml	10fl oz (1/2 pint)	2 litres	3 1/2 pints